Snow Balls

Snow Balls

short stories

Susanna Lee

Rose Mason Press

Douglassville, PA USA

10 9 8 7 6 5 4 3 2 1

Rose Mason Press, an imprint of HPL Publications,
PO Box 564, Douglassville, PA 19518
USA

ISBN: 978-1-61305-033-0

Library of Congress Control Number: 2021952103

Library of Congress Cataloging-in-Publication Data

Lee, Susanna, 1956 –
Snow Balls / Susanna Lee
        p. cm.
ISBN: 978-1-61305-033-0
I. Title
PS3621.S66L44
811'.6-dc23   2021952103

Summary: Close observation captures moments in poetry.

Subjects: Poetry; Poetry -- Authorship; Lee, Susanna --
Poetry; American poetry -- 21st century.

Tags: poetry, American poetry.

Cover photo by Susanna Lee.

Dedication

To all who teach children to read.

Contents

Short Stories (cont.)

Short Stories (cont.)

short stories

A Girl Scout Is a Sister to Every Other Girl Scout

The 23-year-old unwed mother of a two-year-old terror-with-a-temper-like-his-father had no babysitter, so the pudgy, mischievous, wild-eyed imp with the hard head and corkscrew-curly orange hair—and a body full of freckles!—and the cutest grin (with one missing front tooth) —and dimples! —always joined us at our Girl Scouts meetings in the poorly-lit basement of the American Legion while his grandmother tended bar upstairs.

I had my own terror-of-a-little-brother-with-ill-manners at home I was all too eager to avoid at every opportunity, so I was not interested at all in helping to control this tornado of a child. But the other girls, some without siblings (I had seven), took turns holding him and chasing him down and feeding him cookies and giving him hugs and letting him sit in their laps, and allowed themselves to be pinched and smothered in his random, peppered-all-over kisses. They volunteered to follow him around and wipe up his spills and sweep up his crumbs, and hovered under whatever it was he had managed to scramble up on top of this time—and they'd catch him whenever he took a tumble. He never hit the floor or got hurt, not while we were there.

Each girl would give a little shout or squeal whenever he'd succeeded in pulling her hair or kicking her in the shins, but the little boy was entertained and always tolerated and seemed grateful for the attention. He helped his mother to teach us how to love the unlovable, to bear unhappy burdens with patience. To practice kindness; to play, in innocence; and to revel in joy.

Our leader's mother had been widowed young and had raised her daughter among cousins on the wrong side of our town. The girl had fallen in with a bad crowd in her teens and wound up on welfare.

Then, cancer from smoking too young had stolen her voice box. Her eyes always twinkled when she saw us, her girls, arrive for our meeting. She smiled with the entire rest of her face, the side that the surgical scar hadn't marred. It was music, that scratchy, hoarse sound that came from the hole in her throat left by the tracheostomy. She sang Christmas carols with us in July as we cruised through town in her mother's boat on our way to help the homeless or plant flowers for the sick or learn CPR and earn our badges.

Our Girl Scout leader had started her own troop: her one wish, to save other young girls from a similar fate.

My family had just moved in from a rural town, where we had no Girl Scout troop. The privileged girls in my new school had all joined Brownies in second grade when invited by their friend, their leader's daughter. Their leader was a stay-at-home-mom (who'd been "widowed," the term for women who'd divorced abusive husbands on the down-low). Though my new girlfriends vouched for me, this woman would not take one more into her troop—and never a girl whose extended family she did not know personally.

I joined the brand-new Girl Scout troop in fourth grade with the ten other girls who were joining Scouts for the first time—late, for lack of a volunteer who wanted to lead this wayward crew—until my leader took up the challenge, at her grandmother's urging "to do something to help less-fortunate others."

We were never Brownies. We had no history. Few of us could afford shoes that fit, much less uniforms and Girl Scout Manuals and camping trips. Most walked to our meetings, their families too poor to own a car. Some walked quite far, but came even when it rained or snowed.

Our leader taught us compassion and resilience, kindness and love. Forgiveness. Redemption. Inclusion; awareness; and hope.

We were a group of misfits, compared with the only other troop in town, the one that only included girls from good families with long-standing reputations for respectability in our small community. They had all joined Brownies when they were eight. Their leader took them horseback riding and skiing, to the Metropolitan Museum of Art and The Nutcracker Ballet. They hosted fundraisers for the hospital auxilliary and made ornaments for the annual tree-lighting ceremony. Their sashes proudly displayed all the badges that would fit. They paid their dues from their weekly allowances. Their mothers baked sweets for their meetings. They slept over at each other's houses. They shared barrettes and owned the same record albums; they swapped socks and skirts in the school restroom; they took cheerleading and piano lessons; they did each other's homework assignments, just for fun.

When my mother noticed my Girl Scout leader was expecting yet another baby—but had still not gotten married—she told me people were starting to talk, concerned that the leader's poor example might be a bad influence. One of the other girls, who was from a very troubled home, had already gotten pregnant and had to leave school in the middle of eighth grade. To protect their adolescent daughters' reputations, many of the other moms had already pulled them out of the troop.

My mom told me to tell my leader I was too busy with my other activities and did not have enough time to continue to attend Girl Scout meetings.

I cried hysterically as I told this young woman my mom was making me drop out of Girl Scouts. Her face told me she was crushed. When she asked me, "Why?", I could not breathe to repeat the lie.

A Privileged Poet Experiences a Solar Eclipse

People like to brag they have seen a total solar eclipse. It sets them apart from the peons, people chained to their responsibilities without the freedom to pause whenever it suits them, not even to see a "once-in-a-lifetime" event.

It is my sense that every human should have the right to choose to view an eclipse. But, peons do not get vacation days, not even to watch an eclipse. People imprisoned, whether wrongfully or for good reason, are not released when the planets unfold their mysteries. Those caring for others do not abandon their charges at the rotation of floaty things. Soldiers do not stop in their watch for peace, not for anything. Physicists continue to maintain a steady hand on lab equipment, every moment of every day, as if their next coffee with cream and sugar depended on it. And, up until now, I have been too busy at this computer to consider any alternate activities.

The pleasure of watching an eclipse belongs to those who can exercise their right to leisure. Poets without a day job will be watching the eclipse to record in a poem what that's like.

And, as I am a poet, I have made the choice not to join the others in seeing this once-in-a-lifetime event. I will record how it feels to be denied the privilege.

I did not watch this solar eclipse—in solidarity with the working class, the disenfranchised, the imprisoned, the caregivers, the vigilant, and those deliberately kept in ignorance of what time it is and of what time important events are expected to happen. I denied myself one of my privileges and recorded my feelings.

It felt like I was super-extraordinarily privileged. I was able to say no to participating in what other privileged people hold up as a precious opportunity to forget about their responsibilities for a moment, the moment just before they go back to work.

I celebrate my freedom to choose, to choose how I spend every minute, every moment of my life.

A Thing Out of the Ordinary

(fiction based on the true story of a girl you don't know)

You were handsome, older, and wiser—in college already. Yet, you came, with lowly me, to my high school prom?! I didn't know you really liked me that much. Or, did you only ask me because our moms were friends?

You were dashing in your green tux. My friends were all jealous. You and I had matching white roses, mine in my corsage and yours in your boutonniere.

At the after-party, our parents chatted and laughed on your porch. You and I walked through your mom's garden. We talked and talked. We had so much in common.

I showed you how I look up at the night sky, "The moon is smiling bright, full, ripe for wishing … !"

"Huh. Drink your beer."

"I wish this night would never end!"

You showed me a new perspective, "Sure, let's watch the moon, from over here on the grass …."

I laid down, snuggled close beside you. My lips parted. I was full of hopeless expectancy. Would you aim to kiss me, a mere high school kid? If you did, when? Would it be soon?

The June air rubbed my heart raw. You reached down beside me. I laid still, trembling in anticipation.

Giddy, I let you grope me … under my skirt. Your wide-opened lips engulfed my face …

This is not just a kiss.

I swear, I wasn't trying to scream, just breathe. My heart was racing. My deflowering was sudden, unexpected, violent, surprising, and …

Welcomed! You love me!!!

I told you I was saving that for love, and you agreed, it's right, it's true, it's the right thing to do. Me, too, you said. It's what we'd do when we knew we were in love.

That's how you know you're in love. It's what you do to show it, to prove you're in love.

So, you really do love me?! I never knew. But, to do this, you *must*. That's what you do. You agreed. We agreed.

So now I know. You really do love me.

If we're doing this, if we're in love, then it must be … that I love you, too!

But … you're still holding me down with all your strength, your mouth over my mouth, and I can't, I can't breathe …

You held me, held my heart captive—until my realization.

When you let go.

You raised your meerkat head, surveyed the scene with rabbit-darting eyes, zipped up, popped up, and walked away without a word.

I looked up. There was only the moon, not you.

I looked over. There was the porch, filled with laughing people, and you, handsome chin jutted, aiming straight for the back door. You went into the house.

Did anyone else see what just happened?

No one had noticed a thing out of the ordinary.

I lay with my stunned silence.

I recovered my panties in the dark. They were torn. I balled them up, stuffed them, hid them in my fist. How could I hide them? They were new, special this morning.

This was not how it was supposed to end.

I crept home alone. Prom walk of shame, grasping my silence, holding on for dear life.

Sitting on my bed, staring at my corsage. The ribbon limp, lifeless, no longer dancing on my wrist … my hand, held firmly by yours, swaying to the music.

I finger the petals. Still moist and supple … I sniff—for clues. Rose petals, heady, fragrant … lied to me … beauty … betrayal … trust, a mortal wound …

I must destroy them, smash them into mush!

I crushed them, one by one.

Though I twirled and twirled this telephone cord, your call, your explanation, never came. Velvet petals, rolled and rolled between my fingers … finally dried. Brittle.

Dust. Crushed, I hold what's left of the once delicate arm candy. I press the wristlet again, holding it to my nose.
Still, your fragrance lingers, stronger than the rose.

After Our Dog Starts Barking

The dog barks steadily from two-thirty in the morning until I finally get up at three-ten, when I find you sprawled out on the kitchen floor. The last time this happened—and you always promise me this—you promised me that that would be the very last time you would commit suicide. Now I know I can't believe you anymore.

You thought it might be easy to commit suicide by cop, but you haven't broken any laws. So you seek out places where the news says people are getting killed these days. You're not even interested in politics, but you went to a political rally. Why? Were you hoping to commit suicide, killed by a White Supremacist driving an out-of-control pickup truck? Too bad, none showed up.

Then you went up to the mall when it opened and you stayed all day. You took in a movie and stayed for the next showing, too. But no psycho showed up with an automatic, a magazine, and an agenda. When they closed the theater after midnight, you even lingered in the parking lot. I'll bet you were hoping for an unbalanced teenager on meth to show up with his father's hunting rifle. Nope, didn't happen.

You sped on the highway on the way home, probably hoping to get pulled over by a policeman who might disagree with the color of your skin. But, you're white.

The one deer that ran out onto the highway didn't even make it across the shoulder before you sped past it safely.

And, no other cars hit yours, either, thanks to the extra police conducting random stops to get drunk drivers off the road—they know you, they always wave you by.

You got yourself a ticket to be an audience member on The Price is Right. Were you hoping the man in the seat next to you was going to turn out to be a serial killer? Next, you tried "Cake Boss." Then, "Wheel of Fortune." No luck.

Too bad, you're still breathing, so you still have to take the dog out at night when she cries. Like you promised!

You gave up your life-long aversion to religion and started attending services regularly. You're just hoping to be caught in the crossfire, aren't you?

You buy season tickets to sporting events and attend concerts in large outdoor arenas. But you always leave before the event starts, the minute security threatens to check your bag for weapons. I guess no one else with weapons would be able to get in, either, would they?

You went to a local gun show. They tell me you asked directions to the next mass shooting. But, they told you, guns don't kill people, people kill people.

So, you signed up for mahjongg lessons. I'm sure you did it only because you wanted to spend more time around more people. The players are cutthroat, but they only hurt each other's feelings. You cried, a little, but you survived.

You read the fine print on the pamphlets that came with your medications. I bet you plan to not see your doctor if you experience headaches, abdominal pain, dizziness, diarrhea, or shortness of breath, which could be evidence of a more serious reaction, such as stroke, blindness, or even death.

I'm onto you. You waited to pee until you got to the bathroom at Penn Station, and then, you didn't wash your hands. Luckily, you didn't get sick. You went to Flint, Michigan and drank the water. You survived. You went on safari in the African jungle and rode in a Jeep with an open top. Due to the new Zika virus, they'd already sprayed for mosquitoes. No dengue fever for you!

The dog loves it when you take her out at midnight. You know I can't have my beauty sleep interrupted. I get cranky.

You took your son-in-law's advice and smoked marijuana while visiting Istanbul's red-light district. Were you hoping for death by imprisonment under harsh conditions, compounded by insufficient bribery? I'll bet you were surprised when they found your American Express card in your wallet and bought themselves Teslas.

You signed up online for a tour with your college alumni association to visit the Egyptian pyramids. Committing suicide by extremist terrorists using something a little more powerful and sexy than a mere AK-47 would have really made your day, wouldn't it? Too bad for you, the tour was canceled due to threat of terrorism.

The travel agent said your deposit was transferrable for another trip, so you went to Switzerland. You told them you were anxious to try alpine skiing. Did you hope to spin off the trail and smash, head first, into a tree? Dash your skull on a rock in a fall? Collide with a young ski-boarder trying out his Christmas present for the first time, even though he hadn't waited until he had had lessons on ski slope safety? You insisted to the tour guide, who warned you of the dangers of death by either chair lift or cable car accident, that you were indifferent, that either of those would be okay by you. It rained the day of your trip. Stuck inside the ski lodge, you decided to sit on the leather sofa by the cozy fireplace and drink hot cocoa. You spilled some on your lap, but you didn't die of an untreated infection from a burn wound. The cocoa wasn't even hot enough to burn your tongue.

You traveled to the Great Wall of China and brought your ghost writer with you. You read somewhere that if you discover that your roots include dissidents, you can write a best-selling tell-all memoir. You told me we could retire on the profits. Wouldn't that have been convenient for you, to die by having been disappeared? Too bad their government paperwork is all electronic now. They have no record of your grandparents. Those stories your family told you must have been all lies.

You flew to Cuba, probably hoping to commit suicide by openly speaking in public about your opinion on politics. It turns out that now, they love tourists. If you bring American dollars, you can say anything you want.

Since that didn't pan out, you tried the same thing on the New York City subway. You looked for gang members to insult. But the city has gone soft. Now, not even the serial rapists will grope you because there are video surveillance cameras everywhere, and career muggers only gossip about you, laugh at you, and post the interactions on TikTok. They even refuse to steal your wallet. They're high-tech now, stealing money by phishing. Gang members don't use knives or guns anymore to settle scores. They just wait for the police to show up to kill people arguing in public. Again, the police let you down, because you are white. Trying to get someone to look up from their cellphone and argue with you, you wasted another two hours of your life you will never get back.

Not that you wanted that time alive in the first place, since already you have to get up in the middle of the night to take out the dog when she cries, which she does every night, and you can't stand it. You don't want to live in a world where you can't sleep all night uninterrupted.

Having failed with every other attempt on the planet, you invested your inheritance in Wall Street junk bonds. You made enough in profits to afford a ticket to the moon. You're afraid of heights. Your plan was to look out the rocket ship window, hyperventilate, and deplete your supply of oxygen before the return trip to Earth. You did not realize they carry plenty of extra oxygen for medical emergencies. Passengers running out of oxygen is bad publicity for the extraterrestrial tourism industry.

In a last-ditch effort, you traveled up and down the Atlantic seaboard, swimming at every beach. You could have died by shark or sunburn. You probably didn't care which. Whichever came first. But, not even that plan worked. Beach Patrol and EMTs separated you from your dreams, every time.

Mother Nature has always been your friend. You went up to the Adirondacks and went camping. The deer ticks probably would have found you delicious, and you would have died of Lyme Disease. Mosquitos found you first and chased you back to New Jersey.

Since you were in New Jersey anyway, you went to Lake Hopatcong to go swimming. I read in the local paper about the toxic algae. Your last wish would have surely been granted, but beach patrol had fenced off access to the waterfront.

You came home and sat down and googled "ways to die."

You read that a leading cause of death is inactivity, so you decided to commit suicide by sitting in a chair endlessly. You arranged to spend your final hours watching kitten videos, since there is a never-ending supply, and one kitten is cuter than the next. I agree, that would be a great way to go. But the kittens were adorable and the videos were so funny, you found yourself laughing uncontrollably. To your dismay, too late you remembered that "laughter is the best medicine." You have probably added years to your life. So, even if you do nothing else but sit and write poetry from now on, you will outlive our dog.

But, darling, stop, already. You were the one who wanted us to get a dog.

I said, who's going to take her out? I'm too busy, I write full-time, and I can't write if I keep getting interrupted.

You promised me that she would be your dog and you would take full responsibility. You promised to take her out, every time she needs to go.

Even in a snow storm? I asked.

Yes, you said, I'll take her out, no matter what.

Even in the middle of the night?

Yes. You promised.

But now, if you die, she will still have to pee. Who's going to take her out? Me? Don't think it's going to be me!

I thought you loved me.

So, stop holding your breath. Open your eyes, wipe that ketchup off your forehead, and stop pretending you're already dead.

I know you can hear me!

Get up off the floor and take out the damned dog. If I have to do it, I'll lose my train of thought again, and every time I get interrupted, it takes me forever to get my concentration back.

I've been writing for years, and this book should have been done by now. I need to get this book out, so I can get on with my life and do something other than sit glued to this computer all day. If I get interrupted one more time, I'll never get this book done.

If I don't finish it soon, I swear I'm going to kill myself.

All Set for Veterans Day

My great-grandfather was terrified, cold, starving, furious to be separated from his family, armed with a weapon he had no intention of firing, and desperate for home. He was grateful for the banks of earth protecting him on the sides of the foxhole he had dug as enemy fire rang in his ears.

He crouched low and listened to ammunition flying overhead and the occasional screams of felled soldiers who had failed in their scramble across the field.

A body dropped from above and slammed into his shoulder. The impact took him temporarily out of the foxhole and onto his high school football field. The tackle sparked memories, games he'd left behind.

The injured enemy soldier, doubled over on my grandfather's shoulder, hugged his own bloodied leg. He cried, hysterical. Silent, wracking sobs.

My great-grandfather was desperate, and so was this other man, and there was not room for two in the tiny space.

My great-grandfather, a tool-using human, hoisted his army-issued shovel and dug the hole deeper, until it fit both of them.

Then, he kept on digging, until he could lay the man down flat on his back. My great-grandfather, a tool-using human, picked up his rifle—and used it.

He used it to set the man's broken leg.

Amusement Park

Let's sit outside on wet, uncomfortable benches with no back rests under umbrellas with random mist spraying us in the face from every direction. Give us no clue as to when we can leave to drive the three hours home in our wet clothes. And let's wait in line for ice cream in a freezing, air-conditioned restaurant.

Let's all of us speak different languages and engage an uninspired, tired interpreter to neglect us.

Let's use hand signals to communicate across crowds of too-loud strangers, and let each person interpret each hand wave according to his or her own country's customs.

Make sure the piped-in music is pop, unrecognizable, narcissistic and continuous, and is played at decibels which prevent thought.

Let the wind blow and the weather report threaten us with electrocution. Intersperse the chaos of the static coming in over the loudspeaker with public service announcements warning us how to stay safe, in mumbled, unintelligible voices.

Let the sun come out the next day while we stay inside at the outlets and watch others shop, till we drop.

Next time, let's not, and tell the kids' mothers we did.

An Uncertain Death

Today we celebrated my daughter's engagement by buying her a floor-length white dress. Proud to have picked out one on sale, she glowed like a bride determined to become a thrifty housewife. Perfectly poised in her flowing satin gown under the borrowed lace veil, her skin shone, her eyes bright with innocence, her complexion unblemished by any hint of unharnessed lust.

I snapped her photo. She was holding a sign, "I said yes to this dress!"

I would remember how I'd killed her on her wedding dress buying day, by hugging her, at her invitation. "Do you want a hug?" seemed so silly a question. I'd been hugging her at every opportunity since she'd left the womb.

And now, I'd been separated from my children by the pandemic for so long, it hurt as if I'd had my breasts cut off.

I cried, "Yes!"

So. I'd just sold my soul to hold my child close to my heart. I'd had to force from my consciousness COVID-19—the coronavirus, like a coiling cobra, still on the loose at our feet.

I invited everyone back to the house for pizza.

After they all left, I did not wash my hands, hoping I'd die from this virus quickly rather than be eaten, bit by bit, by the guilt. I'd hugged all four of my children, and my only grandchild, to death, all on this one, beautiful day in June.

Appointments Make God Laugh

Sorry, but no, I can't help you with your fundraiser. I know how it looks like I am not busy because I'm home all the time. I don't have a job, at least not one that makes money. But, I am working, and full-time.

As you know, I'm a poet. I have cut back on all my other commitments until I get my poetry book out the door. Although I have been a regular volunteer with you in the past, I hesitate to commit to the date you need me for until I know I am not going to be in a creative spot where the flow of my work will need to continue uninterrupted.

I just need to get this project finished. Put to bed, done.

This kind of work is all-consuming, almost like editing "War and Peace" while rewriting every page and making sure you don't leave out anything important and the story still flows smoothly—

But, doing this while history is being re-written. The results of the DNA tests come back and upset the family lineage of every character. And the computer crashes. The research, carefully compiled as the bones to the story, is from "reliable" sources, who have recently been uncovered as liars and scoundrels. A facial tic has suddenly made its presence known, but there is no time for googling, much less for calling the doctor's office, showing up for an appointment, or filling a prescription.

It's as if I'm a writer, but I still haven't made up my mind about how to present my idea, vacillating between writing a novel, a book of poetry, a series of short stories, an illustrated cookbook, a made-for-TV documentary, or a single haiku which would simultaneously describe succinctly both "war" and "peace"—and I really think I need to add one more word to the title, but I haven't yet decided which. Possibly, something along the lines of "War and *Trees* and Peace"? Although I know, that's not it.

The difficulties in being a poet are complicated. Writing poetry is like, … I'm not sure, but did Armageddon just break out, starting with a backing up of my house's septic system?

I have 1,500 pages of poetry and short stories written, which I am trying to decide how to neatly divide into books of 200 pages, while adding more new stories and poems every day and trying to figure out how to publish them on a budget of zero dollars without any time to devote to finding a person who might be able to help with the twin tasks of computer troubleshooting and publishing online.

It's a lot to keep balanced in my mind. Writing is a continuous-flow process. Finishing a book is a major commitment. I want to see my work on printed pages for my own convenience, so I can find a poem of mine when I want to reread it, if for nothing else.

I know it looks like I don't have a deadline because I have no boss and no editor breathing down my neck. I refer you to my haiku, "Poet's Deadline."

Go ahead. You try to find it. I can never find any of my own poems when I'm looking for them, which is why I need to get this book into print. But, the gist of the poem is, you can only write poetry as long as you aren't already dead, which always seems to happen sooner than one is prepared for. Write now, while you're still breathing. That's always been my motto.

I attend many poetry readings, and often perform at the open mic. To prepare, I spend an inordinate amount of time throwing out everything I have ever written in order to find forty words I can read from a typewritten sheet in front of six people who may not even be still awake and paying attention to what I am saying because they have their own issues: see my poem, "When Poets Come To Hear Themselves."

Every time I open my mouth with a poem, I want to use the opportunity to reassure any listener that they live in a world where love is possible, it actually occurs, it is happening at that very moment, and it will never end—bringing the voice of God to the world is a heavy burden I take seriously. How else would God speak to us, but through each other's lips, His word spoken in the tongue of believers, His message clearly conveyed through careful assemblage of syllables? This is not a rhetorical question.

I know how much your worthy non-profit needs help, and, though I'm busy, I'm considering volunteering with you again because I'll already be at another appointment in the middle of the day, one I know I really should not break. I have been hesitant to make any appointments at all, though I am pretty sure God could use a good laugh. I do have my usual breaks from writing scheduled in, sprinkled throughout the month, usually just book clubs, discussion groups, and choir. My writing is my priority at the moment, so all events have only been "penciled in" on my calendar and are subject to cancellation without notice.

If I am at a meeting and remember a good word for a poem or story I'm working on, I will quietly leave and rush home to make the edit before I forget. If I have not yet arrived and it's late, I'm struggling to find a point in my work where I can take a break without losing forty-eight hours of concentrated effort. I'm on a roll, and I'm writing.

I haven't seen my kids or grandkids for a while. My husband is home here all day, but to him it must seem as if his wife is a ghost. I have skipped events with my sisters. I wear dark glasses to the supermarket so no one will attempt to engage me in conversation.

I have learned how long I can wear one set of clothes before laundering. I write odes to the dust bunnies under my bed. I say, without exaggeration, I no longer brush my teeth on a regular schedule. I bathe when I fear for my health otherwise. I ignore my kitchen, cognizant of the fact that others have endured starvation and survived.

I've penciled in your fundraiser on my calendar and will give you a definitive answer to your request for a firm commitment, but not until the day before the event. If I do promise, I'll come.

I do want to leave some space on my agenda to spend time in the south of France, which I've heard is lovely in the spring, and now is the time to make reservations. I want to go everywhere and do everything fun a person could possibly do in an infinite number of lifetimes.

Why, again, do we each have only one life?

Bukowski's Challenge

I was just trying to enjoy a rare long soak in the tub when Charles Bukowski slipped into my head.

"I'm just trying to help," he complained, as he saw me balk. "Don't you even want to be a poet?" He snarled in disdain.

He wrested the wheel from my death-grip and took me for a spin around my own bathroom. Shit stains confound the toilet. Fart bubbles rise in explosive stench with the bath bubbles.

"There." He pointed it out. The spots of toothpaste on the mirror over the sink form an outline when you connect the dots. "Look closely, it's the shape of love's peculiar thumbscrews."

I didn't want to recall my old lover, one foot out the door, calling me by "her" name, laughing it off, re-gifting me with her disease.

Bukowski chided me to stick to the truth. He reminded me that the viscous blob stuck on the shower wall in front of me at eye level was not the disgusting remains of a dead bug whose half-gutted corpse lay abandoned by an ambitious, but sated, spider.

It's an ever-moist, never-to-be-mouldering, freshly-deposited-daily glob of my husband's sneeze-in-the-shower snot.

Checking in at the Pajama Hilton

After my doctor failed to agree with me that my symptoms of depression, constipation, sinus infection, fatigue, and sleepless nights were being caused by my failing thyroid, he refused to retest me until my yearly exam, which wasn't coming up for two more months. He told me I was being tested often enough and to continue taking my current dose of thyroid medication, which could be increased if the next test showed any changes.

After the doctor loaded me up with antibiotics, painkillers, and decongestants for the sinus infection, I still experienced four days in a row of intense sinus pain and did not sleep at all. After the doctor added Benedryl to the mix, I was left with experiencing a new and unfortunate symptom—delusional thoughts, which could have been due to any number of medical reasons: a failing thyroid, a lack of REM sleep for more than four days, or it could have been a side effect of the Benedryl or any of the other medications he gave me.

Fortunately, I was in good health other than that, and did not smoke or drink or take anything else that might have complicated my condition. However, besides my current medical state, I had just that morning come into a state of near-panic, from something totally unrelated. I was worried sick about my teen daughter. I had just found out that she had done something extremely risky which might have put her in danger of being abducted—with her full cooperation—by a stranger.

She was an impressionable teenager, and had agreed to meet at Disney World someone she had met on the internet. Although we lived in New Jersey, she had an upcoming class trip with her high school band to play in a competition, and the person on the internet had instructed her on how to slip away from her chaperoned group without getting caught.

When I expressed my horror, she added, "I'm going, and you can't stop me!"

My daughter: the rebellious teenager with no common sense, looking for attention. The internet had found the perfect fool.

I was terrified.

The stranger had sent my daughter a videotape in the mail, so my daughter had to have given out our home address. I had watched the thirty-minute tape, which had arrived that morning while she was still at the previous night's sleepover at a friend's house. The video showed four girls, who all looked to be about my daughter's age, fourteen, dancing in skimpy bathing suits outside around an outdoor swimming pool, which the girl in the video said was near Disney World. The girls were singing pop songs and combing each other's hair and putting suntan lotion on one another. They were happily talking about how much they loved smoking pot and being high, how it was great to get to eat all the junk food they ever wanted, and how happy they were to be pregnant with their dreamboats' babies. In the video, they invited my daughter, by name, to join the four of them in Florida, or, if she couldn't get away from home, to at least send them a similar video, encouraging my daughter to videotape herself with three of her friends from New Jersey. In their bathing suits. Dancing.

I considered calling the police. Instead, I waited until my husband got home from work to discuss it. When I told him, my husband immediately went into a state of denial. He said he did not believe that our daughter would do such a foolish thing. He told me he thought I was going nuts, that I sounded hysterical. Yes, I was hysterical. I had just watched the video for about the tenth time. I could barely believe it myself, but there it was. And my husband would not even watch it once, telling me it was crazy even thinking she might do such a thing, that I had to have made it up. But, no, I had the videotape to prove it. He wouldn't watch it. I saved it for five years before finally throwing it out, in case I might have had to prove my sanity to a rational human being.

At that moment, however, I suddenly found myself not thinking clearly. I really was going nuts. But, this was not about my daughter—I was perfectly sure she was an idiot teenager like any other, and I had the facts straight and just had to think of how best to deal with her to keep her safe. But, I became truly alarmed when I started having the delusional thoughts. It was a side effect of my medical condition, I was sure, but the illusions were real. The thoughts were somehow religious … and involved Jesus, or evil, or something … something strange.

I recognized the thoughts as irrational and was petrified that if I lost my mind due to this doctor's malpractice, I would not be able to help my daughter deal with this crisis in adolescent judgment. She might actually run away with the lunatics from Florida I had seen on the tape. All I knew was, I had to keep hold of my sanity in order to help my daughter.

The more I tried to explain to my husband what was going on, the more he was convinced that I was out of my mind. I don't know what led up to his calling 911, but I found myself being taken to the local emergency room at midnight, the police car's flashing lights alerting my neighbors that something was up.

An officer arrived to help, and he talked with me and my husband in our bedroom. As I was still able to reason, he convinced me to put on my bathrobe and sneakers and walk with him downstairs and asked me to allow him to escort me to the hospital. He drove the squad car while I rode in the back seat with my father, who I was just starting to think might possibly be Satan in disguise. On the way to the hospital, my mental condition worsened. By the time I arrived at the emergency room entrance, I believed that the police officer driving the squad car was an incarnation of Jesus.

As we pulled up to the hospital, my dad was reminding me of the current plan we had agreed on, that we would get out of the car together and I would walk into the emergency room with him. I kept thinking he might be trying to trick me into willingly walking straight into hell. I was afraid for my soul. I knew I wasn't thinking clearly, and I was deathly afraid. I did not know who I could trust.

At the police officer's suggestion, we came to a compromise. Rather than walk into the ER, I was able to stay where I was in my seat while they brought a hospital gurney out to the car. I decided it would be safer if I kept my eyes shut, so that God would not think I was willingly walking into hell, if that was what was going on. I decided to not walk at all—but to allow the doctors to take care of me inside the hospital, if we were indeed still based in the real world.

I went perfectly limp, and allowed them to pick me up, put me on the gurney, and wheel me into the ER. My eyes were shut tight. I was hoping for the best, praying that this was a medical team after all, doing what they could to save my mind without hurting my body, and that I was not being carried to my eternal doom by a team of Satan's bad actors.

The ER doctor shot me full of thorazine, or whatever medication it is that they give people when they don't have enough staff to deal with all of the patients who come into the ER at midnight needing immediate attention for their psychiatrtic symptoms. They left me alone in one of the ER rooms strapped to the stretcher.

But, not only was I in mortal terror for my eternal spirit, I was physically in agony from my worsening infection. I tried to alleviate the pressure in my sinuses by turning my head from side to side, trying to use gravity to release the glob of infected tissue from where it felt like it was bursting through my skull, stabbing me in the face from the inside. I was strapped in, laying on my back, and tried desperately to turn myself over onto my stomach, but couldn't maneuver from side to side because of the way the straps constrained my torso on the gurney.

What I did manage to do was to flip over part-way. Half of me fell off, and I dangled precariously, my legs held to the table by the one remaining strap I could not undo.

It took forever for someone walking through the ER hallway to see me and then find a nurse to help get me back up on the gurney. I was able to explain to them how I was in pain and how I needed to turn over on my side to take the pressure off my irritated sinus cavity. They managed it so that I was able to lie down a little more comfortably.

Hours later, when I finally had an interview with the doctor, he told me I needed to check myself into the mental health clinic for an extensive evaluation. It could take up to two weeks. I was lucky a bed had just opened up and my insurance would cover it.

He said that since delusional thoughts can lead to irrational behavior, which can be dangerous, if I refused psychiatric treatment and insisted on going home, they would have to remove my four young children, because they wouldn't be safe staying in the same house with me. He said my dad had agreed that they could stay with him and my mom if I had to be hospitalized. They lived just a few miles down the street. My husband still had to go to work every day.

It was the day before the last day of summer vacation, and my kids would be starting the new school year before I would be able to be home—and I would only be going home if I recovered my mental health.

I was petrified for my kids, especially my fourteen-year-old, who might use the opportunity of having her mother indisposed to do something really stupid. She could wind up in Florida or god knows where else. Even if I recovered mentally, she might never make it back home.

I was still delusional and still wasn't convinced that my dad wasn't, in fact, secretly one of Satan's accomplices. By now, I was starting to believe that my husband most certainly was one of the bad guys. I am lucky the counseling staff was competent. They helped me to evaluate my options and develop a plan back toward mental health. They relayed my concerns about my daughter to my mother over the phone. They helped me to see that I had to let go of my worry over my daughter and trust my mother to handle the situation, because I needed to focus on getting better myself. They weren't really sure yet how ill I was or why.

The doctor I saw at the clinic agreed to test my thyroid. When the results came in a few days later, they agreed with my own original diagnosis. They adjusted my thyroid medication, and, between that and the antibiotics to fight the sinus infection, all my symptoms soon cleared up. I was sleeping normally again, free of pain, and I felt psychologically back to normal. But they insisted the bout of delusional thinking could be symptomatic of an underlying mental health condition. They wanted to do an extensive mental health evaluation, and, just to be on the safe side, they prescribed two different psychiatric medications, for depression and schizophrenia.

I had no idea how these medications might affect my thinking. I realized that my lifelong intermittent bouts of mild depression and anxiety, which were normally under control, were now likely to be aggravated by my taking mind-altering medications. I might indeed lose my sanity. I worried about how long I might be stuck in the hospital. I recalled reading of how

Russian dissidents had been forcibly medicated to make them cooperate, or to just keep them like zombies so they wouldn't interfere with politics.

I knew it was hit or miss, how soon I might be judged "mentally healthy" enough to mother my own children. I really hoped my idiot husband or negligent parents wouldn't ruin them for good before I got home. I was desperate to not lose hope, and I was determined to figure out how to convince the hospital staff I was sane as quickly as possible.

My mother came to visit the second day, and fortunately, I was in a competent state of mind when I calmly explained to her about the video my daughter had received in the mail and how worried I was. I did not tell her I was "desperately worried," though I was. I wanted her to see I was back to normal, to believe I was rational. She told me she would talk to her.

I realized that I'd have to keep my faith in god, to trust that everything would be okay, because I had no other way to protect my daughter and my other kids while I was in the hospital. I had to make a concerted effort to make myself as mentally stable as possible in order to convince the doctors to let me go home. I panicked every time I remembered that there was no guarantee I wouldn't be stuck there for the rest of my life. I cannot remember ever being so frightened.

I was a generally active person, and, now confined to a small wing adjoining the hospital, I knew I'd need to keep up regular exercise to keep fit and sane. I had nothing to read, no family to care for, and I couldn't go running. I did jumping jacks and sit-ups on the floor next to my bed, took long-stride excursions up and down the short hallway, and endlessly circled the main room while trying not to block the view of others watching TV. At home, I carried my eight-year-old twin boys around like footballs when we played. I had to keep up my strength, so I'd be able to resume my normal play with the kids when I got home. I exercised. I ate well. I slept. I talked to the other patients, to see if there was anything I could learn from them, or anything I might be able to do to help them.

I don't remember much about the food, but I do remember how, after three days on the psychotropic medications, in a gesture of goodwill to all mankind, I kissed on the lips a strange man, a fellow patient. I was surprised at how ardently he kissed me back. Fortunately, the nurse on duty was there to help.

Once I realized how the medications were affecting me, I redoubled my efforts to regain as much of my normal state of mind as I could: to sift through the new, overly "happy" inclinations in my mood, and dial them down; to find my true center of gravity, and not allow my "self" to be buried under the effects of the medicines. I prevailed in asking for smaller and smaller doses of the meds, and felt more and more like my old self, though I still had a "floating," or disassociated, feeling, which did not dissolve until I was finally, months later, allowed to discontinue the medications for good.

I did fear for my life at one point while I was in the hospital, at seeing the behavior of another patient. On hearing the angry young man sitting next to me in group therapy describe, in tones of increasing desperation, something which seemed to be meaningful to him, yet sounded illogical and mostly unintelligible to me, though no one else seemed to notice anything unusual about him, I was afraid he might lose it at any moment and attack somebody. I was within easy reach.

He was yelling near the top of his voice. His garbled pronunciation attested to a swelling of his tongue, which I attributed to possibly being a side effect of long-term use of a medication, which I had learned about in one of my college classes in psychology. As he yelled, he gestured wildly with his hands and shook his head violently. His long curls gallivanted across his broad, construction-guy shoulders. He rose to his feet, then repeatedly slammed his clenched fist into the open palm of his other hand, as one demanding justice.

No one else flinched. No one's expression changed in the slightest. I didn't know if they were all medicated to zombie status, or frozen in fear, as I was, or if they knew him and were familiar with him and his behavior and knew him to be harmless in his diatribe. Even the counselor leading the session had a blank look on her face I couldn't read.

I sat frozen in fear, while he ranted and raved and rambled on. Later on, when I asked her, the counselor said it would be okay for me to sit out the sessions if I felt uncomfortable. I stayed in my room after that until he was discharged two days later. But

I stayed on my guard, and now made sure to evaluate each new patient, on arrival, like a pro. I knew insane asylums could be dangerous. The behavior of people who are not in their right minds is unpredictable. People stay here, separated from the general population, for good reason.

I had always been in good mental health, other than some occasional depression and a little anxiety. I was new to the idea of staying in a mental hospital and slow on the uptake about what was expected of me. I had no idea how it worked.

It had taken me only three days, after beginning to sleep well again, to examine my own state of mind and determine I really was psychologically well, but it took another week to figure out the first steps in what I had to do to get back to my family. If I was well, why was I yet being kept in a mental hospital? I had to ditch my trust in the institution. If they did not recognize a person in good mental health when they saw one, I could not predict when or if they would let me go home and take care of my kids.

I tried to discuss with the doctor the religious delusions I had had, trying to get answers as to the cause and whether I should be concerned, but as soon as I spoke, I saw him record my words in his notes. Whatever I had said during the session before came back at me again at the next succeeding visit, evidence enough for the doctor to support a diagnosis that I was continuing to suffer ill mental health. I decided to keep to myself any continuing concern over my past delusional thoughts and eliminate all candor in discussing the possibility that I had any lingering symptoms.

I was fine.

The doctor told me how lucky I was to have good health insurance. They could then concentrate on whether or not I needed continued care rather than be forced to send me home too early out of fear the hospital would not be reimbursed for a lengthier stay if I needed one. I suspected that it was a complication with his insurance coverage that had led to the dismissal of the angry young man. He had stayed for only a few days.

To the doctor, I expressed my concern for the countless others I knew were out there, outside the doors of the hospital, suffering with mental illness, just waiting for a bed that could accept them so they could get treatment. I told him how guilty I felt, taking up a bed, when so many were ill and beds were so scarce. I wondered aloud about the raving gentleman, and how he had left after only two days. He didn't seem at all well enough to be considered recovered, at least, not to me. I hoped he was safe at home with his family, and, I joked, I hoped his family was safe, at home, with him back.

I joked with the staff that, if I were in their shoes, since they had a limited number of beds, if they were given a choice of clientele, I'd keep me as a patient as long as I could. I was not dangerous, did not scare the other patients—like some of the other patients did—and I felt I was rather pleasant to chat with.

It turns out, they did keep me as long as they could—the insurance stopped paying after two weeks and they sent me home that day.

They did not pronounce me "cured."

Christmas Eve

We start baking on Christmas Eve as soon as the last person arrives. We use the same cookie cutters every year and decorate from our stash of green and red sugar crystals, tiny colored dots, chocolate sprinkles, and cinnamon hearts. Each person gets to pick which cookie they want to leave for Santa. Don't forget the glass of milk and a carrot!

We sit together on the couch and admire the freshly-cut Christmas tree we had earlier agreed was "perfect" before we tied it to the top of the car and hauled it home. It sits upright in its stand in front of the picture window, its blinking lights declaring to the neighbors—our family is on holiday. The tree is now plugged in and aglow, covered in tinsel, and decorated from the box in the basement with red and blue balls, green garlands, and ornaments: some boughten, some sewn, and some made of macaroni glued to cardboard and spray-painted gold. Our tree-topper is is a star outlined in colored lights. It's cheap, from Walmart. Walmart always has an identical replacement in stock.

We all sit on the couch and take turns reading aloud the verses of "A Visit from St. Nicholas." Then we sing, a cappella, all the Christmas carols we know. Our "Christmas Elf" sneaks into the kitchen and fills up the stockings to overflowing with fresh fruits, candy, a Pez dispenser, and one special little present: a Duncan yo-yo, a pack of Bicycle playing cards, a dreidel, or a tiny Slinky. A candy cane and a banana peek from the top of each stocking. After the last verse of the last song, we munch out on the cookies, drink up the milk, and take turns taking bites to crunch up the carrot. We ignore the filled stockings, that have already mysteriously appeared on the hearth, and the tons of wrapped presents, already, magically, under the tree. These treasures, we will "discover" in a few hours, when we wake up—at home!—on Christmas morning.

Whenever you wake up, you can eat what's in your stocking.
But don't touch the gifts before mom's up.
And don't wake her before six.

Cold Shower

When I was invited to a family party, I asked my husband to explain my in-laws' gift-giving expectations.

"Your sister's daughter is having a baby! Can you help me think of a traditional gift she might like that I could bring to the shower?"

"No gift. We only give money."

The man I married, who had promised me on our wedding day he only wanted to be American from now on, is now, in his dotage, his Taiwanese father, scolding his Chinese wife, "That's not our custom."

As if I should know.

"That's only American. We don't give gifts. And, not now. They don't even have the baby! When a baby is born, that's when we give money. That's our way."

This explains why I've never received a gift. Not for Christmas, not for my birthday, Valentine's Day, our wedding, anniversary, or "just because." I thought it was because we were so poor that we never shopped for an engagement ring. We wouldn't even have had wedding rings, had not an artist friend given us rings as a present. We never had a honeymoon and never took a vacation, except for two days at Disney with the kids, and that was educational, just so they would at least have had the experience of having ridden in a airplane and stayed in a hotel. They were in their teens.

As is the custom in "his" culture, my husband does his duty. He goes to work. He puts all of his money into our joint account. I shop. He doesn't buy anything.

When I buy him a gift, he complains. He says, go ahead, you can buy anything you want for yourself. Just don't buy anything for me.

Everything he has, he says, belongs to me. All the things in our house. All the money in our bank account. "It's all yours." Generosity is the highest form of love.

And, of course, I love him. So, vice versa. Because I love him, I have nothing I can call my own. It's all his.

So, why would I use his money to buy him a gift?

And, I can't give him money. How could I give him something that's already his?

Combat the Wombat

The latest project of the Sierra Club, "Combat the Wombat," generated 87 million signatures on its moveon.org petition and raised $294 million on kickstarter. The poster with the baby wombat's photo was simply adorable—irresistible! Street vendors couldn't print counterfeit t-shirts fast enough.

What was it that had caused the outcry, the demand that wombat babies be rounded up and incarcerated in zoos? Wombats seem so harmless, so cute in pictures. Our local TV reporter could find no one to interview who could identify a single grievous fault in any baby wombat. Incomprehensible!

The Sierra Club—usually so in tune with matters of fur and feathers—today, on the side of . . . politicians!?! It must be a cadre of scheming foreign oil barons, or a homegrown cabal of those steeped in the dark arts, or some other weirdos, members of one or the other of the various nefarious groups who have succeeded, at last, in finding the perfect terrorizing tool, one that could strike directly at the heart of all that was American. Aimed with precision to destroy our confidence in self-fulfilled destiny, they hit their target bullseye: our humanitarian identity.

No! Impossible! It must have been a computer error. Neighbors console one another, "Ain't that the truth! It's always the damned computers."

And, in the balance, lay the fate of baby wombats. Wombat mothers teetered in hysterical passion. Wombat fathers, helpless to rescue their own, exhausted themselves in anger and frustration.

There exists, in the deep pools of baby wombat eyes, a precious glimmer, beautiful as the glow on unstained, fresh-licked lips below a pair of young human eyelids tainted from their first brush with purple glitter.

Dad Begs Me for a Knife

The Alzheimer's patient could not remember those tubes were in his body for a reason. The fluids pouring in would keep him alive if he gave this treatment a chance.

He tugged at the wrist restraints like a drunken sea captain resisting a mutiny: caged below in the brig, shouting and cursing and rattling his chains; determined to wrest back control of his ship, of his seamen, his crew, his cargo, his rum, his wench, his destination, his destiny. If he couldn't murder the mutineers, he, the captain, would go down with his ship!

If he could survive being tied to a bed for a week, he would have a chance for a less painful death, a chance to be spared agony—for a little while longer. Dad felt fine. Healthy. Strong. Furious. He could not remember he was sick with lymphoma or why they were keeping him restrained in a hospital bed. What in God's name were the doctors doing to his body?

And where was my mother, his loving wife? She would never have allowed such a thing! "What have you done with my wife!?!" The thought was unbearable. He cried. He sobbed. He screamed in heartbroken agony.

Our dual helplessness was inexplicable and fathomless. Without understanding, there is no consent. He could not comprehend there could be any reason at all he should be subjected to interventions. He could no longer argue well enough to convince his kidnappers that he really meant it: "No! dammit! Cut me loose, or kill me now!" Willing to be disowned and damned for not bringing him a knife, I stayed by my dad's side until the crisis had passed and they removed the straps, so thankful he would not remember my betrayal.

I'd once held a screaming newborn—in pain and disbelief that, I, her mother, had made the world so: hell, with no relief.

Danger Underfoot

When my children were toddlers, I taught them that if they found a candy fallen on the floor in the supermarket or on the sidewalk or even in our own kitchen, they should not eat it!

Give it to me, I explained. It might not be a candy, it might be something dangerous, pretending to be candy. And I will trade you a real candy for it.

Kids must alert a grownup if they see a candy on the floor. Let the grownup pick it up and see what it is. It might be candy, or it might not be. If it's candy, it's dirty from being on the floor. Either way, the grownup will make sure it won't hurt anyone, especially another child, who might not know *not* to put it in their mouth—just don't eat it!

But it has got to be picked up. Whatever it is, it might hurt someone. You never know . . . .

I will trade you a real candy for anything you find anywhere, on the floor or laying around anywhere else, if it looks like candy. Even anything that just looks shiny and looks like it might be candy, but isn't candy. We called those imposters "candy-*looking* shinies."

Whatever I gave them, they could eat with my permission. And I let them destroy all of the imposters, the candy-*looking* shinies, by flushing them down the toilet.

My toddlers loved to flush the toilet! When they threw a candy-*looking* shiny in the toilet and flushed, we always laughed and celebrated!

The candy-*looking* shiny did not kill us—this time.

Dead, Unclothed, and Abandoned

"Dead, Unclothed, and Abandoned"

—*local newspaper headline*

My heavy cotton sweater keeps in my warmth, even as I open the front door to freezing temperatures. I let the puppy outside for his morning pee.

He runs to get back inside, but not because he is cold or wants to keep me from freezing—and he is not expecting a treat—but he likes to play Keep Away, and he knows we will.

The only glow is from the computer screen. I'm almost inured to headlines.

The dead baby's mother has not been found.

Stem cells from cord blood may be collected immediately after birth and frozen for medical use, but the blood in this frozen, uncut umbilical cord will not be preserved to help another child stay alive.

An ad for a cord blood collection service in the column next to this article touts using vapor nitrogen over liquid nitrogen. Infections or bacteria can "swim" through liquids and infect other cord blood specimens.

Who knew?

I've read enough for one morning. I look up, to see the sky, through my picture window, explode—dawn pink.

Dear Anton, I Borrowed the Last Line of Your Poem . . . But, Here, I Brought It Back—Oh, No! Now It's Wrinkled, Sorry

Every morning I go outside to fetch the newspaper from the letter box. Birds are already lined up on the telephone wire between the poles, waiting for Anton's last line to lead them in song. But, it's missing!

I read the newspaper. Paterson Falls is dammed. It splutters and jams. Its water is piled up, an ocean ladder reaching to the moon. The river refuses to fall, waiting for Anton's last line to drop first.

I put down the paper and pick up the phone, to warn others. I'm late. Five-year-olds at the neighbor's birthday party last night swung their bats, but their swats could not break the piñata. It refused to share its sweets before Anton's last line showed up. It never did.

I look out the living room picture window, and realize the tree in the front yard is not casting a shadow. The sun has decided to wait to shine, until Anton's last line decides to visit.

I turn on my computer and check social media. It's the same everywhere. Facebook. Twitter. BBC World News. TikTok. Everyone is drowning in tears. Anton's last line is missing. I turn on the evening news. Arctic glaciers bob fiercely on the roiling sea, pleading for the safe return of Anton's last line.

I can't bear it. I turn it off.

The disaster drags on for weeks and weeks. Lawnmowers go to sleep, unneeded, as grass rends itself, distraught without Anton's last line. The earth opens up and swallows its own dust in fear that Anton's last line has come to a bad end. Is there no hope?

I turn on my printer. It's saved me, in the past.

The heroic machine revs up—it shoots out one black duplicate of Anton's last line!

Please, Anton, take it. I forgot I'd borrowed it.

Hold tight to your poems, Red Wheelbarrow Poets, hold tight.

Dingman's Falls

These rocks were once formed by spurting volcanos, and each had its own colors burned in.

Earthquakes pushed boulders to new heights. Water has dogged the irregularly-shaped, massive structures for eons, wearing them smooth with constant streaming, relentless rushing. Hard formations still exist on this mountain, as rocks; still resist the demands of gravity to give water full right of way. Rocks refuse to give in to calls for their own reform. Transformation would ultimately mean destruction.

Flowing down crooked paths, water did not ask to be released from its underground haven. Thrust out, high up, into the spotlight, water rides with gravity, seeking its own level, just as pickup trucks seek an empty parking spot at the meeting hall where flowing beer etches away at logical thinking on the twin topics of politics and sex.

Water! There's no reason to maintain a low profile, says the sun. The sun often lends its power to lift water, one molecule at a time. Water is encouraged to liberation.

As water, propelled from its underground font, spills out onto the hills, it splashes rocks. Its drops separate into mist.

The sun rises to lend water, a lens, light, in which to share its vision of freedom. A rainbow soon spans the rocky cliffs. Its broad grin laughs at the persistence of gravity, still trying to draw all water down below the level of rocks.

Rocks, sitting on top of the ground everywhere at Dingman's Falls, might as well be hiding underground as below this rainbow. Much as logic fails to attract the notice of those bedazzled by political chutzpah or product advertising, no one present sees any rocks at all.

The rainbow is blinding in its beauty.

Displaced Persons

Their first day in the new neighborhood. They'd just unloaded the last load from the pickup truck.

Snow started to fall. Big flakes. Swirling. Then, heavier and heavier, more and more snow. A real nor'easter. The snow accumulated to two feet. High winds knocked out the power, downed trees everywhere.

No electricity. No phone, no TV, no internet. No heat. No water. No car. The driveway was blocked with downed trees. They were stuck in the dark in the cold: the dad, the mom, and their six-month-old baby boy. And, it was still snowing.

For three days, workers cleared felled trees from driveways. Two days more before the road was all cleared to the highway. But still, there was no power. No heat. And no water.

So, they got out. Holed up in a motel. As their one credit card maxed out, another snowstorm roared in.

Six days later, the bridge was finally re-opened so they could get across the river and get back to their jobs. Two days later, the electricity came back on at home.

Home. They were home, at last.

They'd begun to get a glimmer of what it must be like for war-displaced persons.

But, they weren't even close. For one thing, nobody had died.

Doggo Storm

When it rains, my Shih-Tzu trembles and cowers in his little, round, plaid green L.L. Bean doggie bed. Though bone-dry, safe and warm in his master's house, he feels threatened by every chance of precipitation. He is roused to primal fear, to mortal terror, by a summer shower. Or fog. Or a cloud. Or snow, sleet, or any hint of moisture in the air. His little purebred ear canals swell with a change in the barometric pressure. The lining of his tiny snout reacts to the unbearable press of his membranes, swollen with the advent of the dew.

A slight drizzle or a bit of humidity might presage a looming threat from nature. His most primitive instinct tells him: lightning and thunder exist!—How close the poor, sensitive pup is, to death!

The appearance of the invisible airborne water-beast scares him silly. He cries all night, all day, whimpering continually . . .

. . . until he realizes, once again, the inflammation in his sinuses has resolved!

His ears are dry. The threat of raindrops has gone.

He's fine. He calms. He's quiet.

How clever, the ancient sages, to breed these living weather stations, to live in the palace and serve the emperor.

Dreaming of Poetry, But Not Walking With Walt Whitman While Awake

Too sick to go out, I missed the Whitman reading. I had chicken soup and toast and retired early at seven-thirty. As the pillow softened my head's fall, Walt Whitman was there, stretched out across my bed with me.

I dreamed I wandered these hills where I live, taking photos with Whitman. I was not sick in bed, missing poetry, missing leaf-peeping season. I dreamed in color of Walt's brown felt hat and pipe and the falling autumn leaves. We shot landscapes and close-ups, twigs and berries, bugs, snakes, ferns, moths, and clouds.

I described to Walt my first car, how, when I'd crashed it into a ditch, the bubble shape of the hood of the white VW bug flattened like the nose of a boxer after losing too many fights.

We compared our approaches to composition, discussed natural lighting versus studio techniques, perspective and depth of field, pheasants, cowbirds, my observation of Robert Frost's love of birch trees—Walt's opinion was that it was either laziness or lack of imagination that sharpened Frost's focus on that one species.

I got a good shot of a fawn, still with the spots of a newborn. Walt said he'd hung in his living room a watercolor of a family of deer, the mother nursing and the stag standing guard. He'd been intrigued by the white flag tails of three does dashing away across a grassy field in the painting he didn't buy. He explained to me what he meant by "singing" America. I explained how I hate jumping spiders, but love how, in photos, dewdrops outline spider webs in lines of white balls. The whites are always blown out, a no-no according to my photography club. Walt told me you can find beetles hiding just under the outer layer of bark if you bring your pocketknife with you on a walk in the woods.

Whitman never leaves home without his. I haven't owned one since I was in Girl Scouts, but in science class in fifth grade, we learned about the lifecycle of beetles and how a tree defends itself with its bark.

Neither Walt nor I ever try to flush rabbits hidden in the brush. They dart away faster than we can bring a camera to eye level.

I showed Whitman how easy it is to frame and crop using the Snapseed app on his iPhone. He was eager to try it. We both agreed, who has time anymore for Photoshop?

We plotted stopping at Starbucks on the way back. We'd order lattes, switch phones with each other and write ekphrastic poetry after swiping through the photos we'd just taken. Poems would spring forth effortlessly, fruits of four thumbs pressing smartphone buttons all afternoon, taking shots and recording visions inspired by a fellow poet. I would forever cherish these works created on my journey with Whitman, photos and poems prepared in my dreams.

But, I woke.

I will not be writing poems inspired by photos taken in dreamland with the poet. Those images are gone and, with them, inspiration for waxing poetic on my town, my woods, my car, my America. I have no selfies with Whitman, with him sticking his tongue out, nor videos of us laughing and singing "Oh, Susanna!" or of him pointing out to me, after looking up, the hawk's nest he saw in the crook of the elm, or his explaining that the hawk is his favorite bird of all because he dreams of seeing their pips break through their eggs while they're hatching—but the nests are too high up and will always be out of reach. How that famous photo of him with a butterfly was of a dead butterfly, and, though his editor had set it all up because he thought the photo would sell books, and it did, Walt would really rather have preferred to not touch the dead thing, and he had washed his hands afterwards.

And while he was talking dead butterflies, I brought up the Cornell Labs Bird Cams site on my iPhone. I showed Walt his pipping hawks.

The l look I saw on his face is what woke me.

I had not been strolling through the woods, knowing I was conversing with a poet, each of us observing the environment as we crashed through it, disturbing its denizens, each hearing and understanding it in our own way, then sharing our experiences.

Pouring from our eyes, from one's pair into the other's?—nothing.

No leisurely walking around, talking. No taking photos of where I live, with an extra poet handy, one willing to generously give me a new perspective.

It never happened.

Edison, Selfish Monster, Missed His Own Child's Baptism

Thomas Edison got by on two hours sleep so he could invent something to allow himself to see in the dark. Successful creative work driven by a dream demands one's full attention. What would you have given to explore the possibilty of inventing a light bulb?

Edison's wife made it possible. She made her family's candles, meals, clothing, and excuses to the children for why their father was seldom seen. The Edison patriarch had no opinion to offer the town council regarding the proposal to disallow gambling on Sunday afternoons. Mrs. Edison smiled at the preacher Sunday mornings. Next to her in the pew, she saved a space for her husband—it was never filled.

My sister-in-law enjoys a financially-secure retirement, leisure allowed by her genius husband's hard work. While my brother-in-law was at the university, enduring the accolades heaped on successful academians, his wife did not complain to him over lost dinner hours. She'd have preferred the whole family seated, engaged in pleasant conversation about the struggles of eighth-grade algebra, the neighbors' divorces, the rising cost of gasoline, and her own mother's rising battle with dementia.

Her husband would not be attending the woman's club's dinner-dance fundraiser to cure Alzheimers'. He was kept in ignorance of his teen son's fender-bender they could not afford to repair. When the high-school band took their trip to Montreal, my brother-in-law never knew they had been looking for more chaperones.

The man never held a Little League baseball, bat, or mitt. He never appreciated how much longer the lines were at the cheaper supermarket, or how drugs were stealing the next generation, or that his own child could not escape the lures that entrapped his peers. He was never told.

He had no time for the drama that circumscribed the life of his wife and adopted son. He worked. He worked on solving the problems of physiology, deciphering mysteries.

He inspired a team of researchers, as Edison did, to work and work and work. They struggled long hours, trying every conceivable combination of possible solutions to replicate the functions of the kidney.

He wasted three hours in combat with his teen son. The tattoo he had forbidden, a fait accompli.

What more work could have been done in three hours?

His son, on reaching adulthood, proclaimed a new-found identity. He came out as a "Black man"—doomed to be forever relegated to the fringes of society, never to be fully assimilated, because of his non-white race.

The scientist had not a clue as to how this could have happened. Wherever could his son have picked up such an absurdity? Didn't he see his father's success? His father, though adoptive, looked just like him, yet he had never struggled with anything more than finding solutions. He had reveled in joy at his opportunities. He had led by example, the epitome of good character. The immigrant—who had successfully navigated the country of irregular verbs and Christmas lights—rent his clothes and gnashed his teeth and fought with his son and did no work for two weeks.

What more work could have been done in two weeks!

My sister-in-law recalled her own work, how she had respected the traditions and had not shamed her husband by letting him know his wife needed to take on a job at a travel agency nor how his son cried every single time she dropped him off at day care. Her family, living in a college town, would have saved money if they could have moved to a less-expensive neighborhood, but they had to stay near campus to keep her husband's commute time to a minimum. They were tethered to his ivory-tower salary. Yes, they needed things. Her son needed a soccer uniform and cleats. They ate shad roe on New Year's. She made it happen.

She saved her worries over the rising prices of household necessities, to share with me in long telephone conversations and at family gatherings, where we commiserated over missing husbands, consumed by their work.

ERA

"In any era, the greatest rarity for women is to be able to control their time."

—Sarah Ruden, first woman to translate
The Aeneid into English (2009)

"People need a social, institutional and economic structure that enables their work."

—Emily Wilson, first woman to translate
The Odyssey into English (2011)

In keeping with tradition, I took two years out of my busy life to sit and play video games and do nothing else.

No, I made that up. The part about tradition.

Okay, I'm a little older than those who usually play video games.

And, isn't it usually men, rather than women, who are entitled to do exactly as they please?

I would like to acknowledge my husband, for keeping food on the table and clean towels in the linen closet and for going to work every day to pay the bills and for continuing to never notice there was anything about me that was out of the ordinary. He remained, throughout it all, unaware of my video game indulgence.

This allowed me, a post-menopausal, post-corporate-America married mother of four, who had worked extremely hard, up until that point, at the "normal" occupations and had accomplished so much, much better worth immortalizing—especially my volunteer work; and my nursing of my twins for three years—to take a break, during which time I was able to change the course of history, if this was, indeed, the first time a woman did nothing but play video games for two years.

I proved that such an act of individualism and self-determination in defiance of societal norms could be accomplished by a woman.

Unless I am lying. Which I am not.

The evidence for this incredible feat is now recorded, preserved for posterity, here in this poem.

I lied. I didn't really do nothing else except play video games for two years.

While I played video games—and I played exclusively on my cell phone, and only free versions: only Sudoku, Solitaire, and Mahjong—my mind was free to contemplate the demands placed on women by society. While my hands were busy with the idle chatter of gaming, my mind was free to work.

Had the video gamer in this story been a man, I would have assumed that while his hands were busy at the controller, he was either actively engaged in the pursuit of happiness or was wasting time, shirking his responsibilities. Would he have listened, had I tried to talk him into using his time more productively or less selfishly?

As a woman, I can't help feeling that I am, right now, being judged. Maybe by you.

You might ask me why I did not at least keep my hands busy in knitting blankets for veterans or newborns or patients in nursing homes. I would have told you I could not afford the possibility I might get distracted from this important work. Examining and understanding society's faults, starting with misogyny, is the first step toward the liberation of humanity from all evils.

Feeding the Body

The turtle, hungry for the tasty plants at the bottom of his pond, takes a deep breath and holds it.

Despite air's threat to keep him buoyant and afloat—away from his meal, his delight—he measures his lung's depth against the heft of his own weight and is confident. Mere air is no match for his mass. He'll sink.

He paddles the rest of the way down until his toes touch bottom. He eats his fill. With every bite, he becomes heavier, more able to command the deeper and deeper recesses of his culinary world.

Yet, he does need to surface, again and again, to take in fresh air. It is necessary to the process of living, to step away from the table, to take care of the business of breathing before rejoining the banquet, the feast.

He hates to have to desert his delicacies to swim up for air. He sees the summer sun taunting as it broadens the leaves at the bottom of the pool. There in the deep are the greens he desires.

The buffet set for him is replenished. It waits for him to gulp more air, dive down, and dig in, again and again, day after day, year after year.

Field Notes for My Cat

Daisy has been dead now for fifty-two years, but she always loved a spontaneous performance. She cheered, in her own little "cat" way, while lolling in the sunbeam. She hung back and allowed the star to take center stage. It was all good, so long as she didn't have to move.

Daisy was an epicure of the finest dimensions. She dropped a yellow bird on the doorstep and apologized for having nibbled at its neck rather than having deferred to our own enjoyment of the rare treat.

Crickets marred her breath whenever birds and tuna were not catchable and anytime crickets appeared, whether other game was in season or not.

There is little more foul than cricket breath on a cat, and that includes the smell of poopy diapers. We had lots of poopy diapers at our house. The oldest of eight kids, I shook my share of goopy, poopy, cloth diapers into the toilet, swirling and swirling, hoping the poop would drop off or stick to the bowl, or at least not keep sticking to the diaper. I don't remember how or if I removed the post-poop soggy diaper from the water, whether I wrung it out, dropped it, stinking, sopping wet, into the bathroom sink, then flushed, or if I slipped it over the edge of the toilet seat and let it fall into a pail to wait for mom to take care of it.

"Diaper pail" was a thing, but I forget the details.

I forget all the details of my life. I always had the idea that I could learn anything but I didn't have to remember anything specific, that I could always look up in the library whatever I'd forgotten, and that none of what I had already learned or experienced would ever need to to be recalled exactly as it happened—not to justify an opinion, nor to serve as a framework for a current project, nor as the basis of a story to tell a child.

There was, and always would be, something new to take its place, something coming after, that would be more important, that would matter, that would require the full psychic energy of my brain and an empty space therein in which to dance, and whatever was already in there would all be pushed aside, effortlessly—whatever it was that I had already done or learned—when, then, my life commenced.

When I would become a poet or a mom or a monster or a clam or the moon.

It did not matter. What I was. What I did. Nothing mattered. No one noticed.

Something would happen.

In the future. I was sure of it, something would happen, and my life would start. From that point on, I would fill my empty brain with all the wonderful things that would happen. My hope chest would be full, with an untouched trousseau, paper and crayons enough to draw an endless universe.

Fly

Dmitri opened the screen door to let out the fly he had just caught and cupped in his hands. It did not belong in the house, and neither did the four flies which had just made their way in as he took that one out.

Flies had been basking in the sun on the outside of the screen door. Startled awake when he jiggled the handle, they began a meandering buzz, scooting in under his elbow, over his head, and between his knees. The one fly to fail to make an entrance into the foyer was the one Dmitri was able to shake free from his palms and fling out over the stairs before scooting himself back inside and quickly shutting the screen door in its fly face.

The four little fly friends now inside gleefully ran amok and set about exploring. They hoped the house would prove hospitable. Even if all the BLTs had already been eaten, perhaps a drop of bacon grease might not yet have been mopped up, or a crust of toast might not have been snapped up by the dog, or a dribble of beer from the master's lip or a tiny splash of milk from one of the toddlers' wobbly cups or one of the teardrops fallen from the corner of one of the mistress's eyes might not already have been lapped up by the cat.

Fourth Grade Creative Writing

For our final project, we had to write and read aloud an essay describing, of all those hobby collections we owned, our most prized. We were encouraged to bring it in to show to the class—our most glamorous Barbie dolls and our electric trains with the most bells and whistles. Whatever it was we collected, we were to tell the story of when and how we came into possession of each piece and why it held a special place in our heart.

All the toys in my house, I shared with seven younger siblings. All were broken. The dolls were naked and nearly bald, as my mom did not bother to lock up her scissors.

I imagined my fellow fourth-graders showing off collections of embroidered lace pillows gifted them by maiden aunts, or describing how their uncles had taught them to use a jigsaw to cut out pieces for their birdhouses. I was sure my neighbor would bring in her collection of silver spoons and relate the stories I had heard her tell of her grandmother's world cruises. She had teaspoons from everywhere: England, France, Greece, Italy— even China and Russia—which she took pride in pointing out on the globe that sat on the white painted desk in her bedroom. The desk was part of a matching set of furniture which included a bookcase, a dresser, a vanity, and the headboard for her bed, all decorated with ornate curlicues and delicate blue flowers. The fabric of the full-sized bed's sheer floor-to-ceiling canopy matched her Princess Pink down comforter and the bedroom's frilly curtains. The shag throw rug was a complementary shade of slightly darker violet. Her mother had let her pick out the Disney throw pillows for herself as a souvenir when they were there on winter vacation with her cousins.

I had brought back a seashell from my family's summer vacation at my cousin's house at the shore, but it had quickly disappeared when I forgot to bring it down to the basement and put it on my desk right away.

My neighbor and I always played outside unless it was raining. Her mother made us wipe our shoes on the outside mat before coming in and leave them on the other mat inside the front door and go straight to her daughter's room, where we sat on the throw rug, not the carpet. My friend had screamed when I sat on her bed the first time I had come over. She and her sister had been strictly instructed to never muss up their carefully smoothed blankets. They made their beds first thing when they got up. Their mother never offered us snack, since they ate dinner every night at six-thirty when her father came home from work and children were expected to have a good appetite. My neighbor would always refuse snack at my house—she couldn't risk her mother noticing she couldn't eat as much as she usually did.

At my house, my family ate supper at exactly five o'clock and we kids were bathed and in bed by seven. My mother ran a tight ship because she and my dad both worked full-time and both were also working on their doctorates. Mom had to stick to a schedule to get everything done, so if any of us missed supper, we were sorry until breakfast. I never missed a meal.

Though I had my own wall lamp for reading in bed during the day, I had to carefully arrange myself under the covers if I wanted to read late into the night. If one of the five sisters I shared a room with complained to my parents they couldn't sleep because a bit of my lamplight had escaped and had nipped them between the eyelashes, my flashlight would be confiscated until morning.

I thought of my classmate, three houses over, sitting at her beautiful desk and writing her spoon collection essay at her leisure—her mother cleaned up the kitchen after dinner so her daughters could be spared evening chores and focus on their homework. My friend's graceful, precise handwriting was the result of countless hours of practice, to please her demanding mother, who proudly sent off in the mail her graded schoolwork to her elderly relatives, who would hang it on their refrigerators.

I didn't have a spoon collection handy. What else could I write about for my essay? I knew I'd have to read it aloud in front of the class, and I didn't want to be embarrassed.

A collection. There was only one thing that I owned more than one of—I had several books. But a stack of paperbacks hardly qualified as a "collection." Who would laugh at me if I called "collecting books" my hobby? What kind of a story could I tell about how I added each of my books to my "book collection"? Books are stories themselves, stories that sit on a book shelf during the day and come to life at night under a blanket.

Yet, I had nothing else. And I did prize the pile I had on my desk and jealously guarded. I would not let my siblings touch a page, for fear it would be ripped or crayoned over or the volume lost. I read the same treasures over and over and slaved at housework, earning my nickels and dimes, in anticipation of the next issue of Scholastic News with its listings of new books. I waited with bated breath for the glorious day a pile of order forms would appear on the corner of the teacher's desk, anxious to peruse the offerings and fill out the precious lines with the titles I lusted for, eager to cash in my dishpan hands for wild dreams.

My mother found me a large paper shopping bag, a treasure chest big enough to haul my hoarded paperback loot to school. As I struggled with my essay, trying to turn "a stack of used early reader books that I was rapidly growing out of" into "the prized collection of an enthusiastic hobbyist and budding bibliophile" that would suit a critical audience, I learned what it means to be "a creative writer."

I started out my class presentation with a little joke about how indulging in my joy for reading left me with little time to play with toys, so, since I didn't really have enough experience with toys to know which ones I prized the most, I had decided to call my books "toys" and bring them as my "toy" collection. Nobody seemed to appreciate my vague attempt at levity to justify the fact that I did not follow the directions for the assignment very closely.

As I took each of my fourteen paperbacks out of the paper bag, I waved it with dramatic flair, showing off the covers. I surprised myself with the passion in my extemporaneous book reviews. But no one else cared.

After I ran out of books, I made another attempt at humor. I described how I drooled over the Scholastic Book Club catalog every month and how I was so desperate to earn money to feed my book habit, I had started asking for more chores to supplement my thirty-five-cents-a-week allowance. My mom paid a nickel to sweep the stairs to the basement; a dime to vacuum the living room rug. I told the class how much I hated the smell of Spic and Span, but washing the kitchen floor paid a whole quarter.

No one heard me. The classroom was silent, bored to tears and staring into space.

All except my teacher, who was thrilled that a student of hers had espoused a love of reading, and, in front of the whole class! She complimented me on my unusual choice of "books" for the subject of my "prized collection" essay, as she chided the rest of the class to follow my example and develop a love of reading. I was never so happy to be able to sit down and melt into my desk and disappear.

My neighbor's mother brought in the spoon collection and arranged it on an embroidered linen towel spread on the teacher's desk. She packed up the spoons again after her daughter's presentation—wiping down each one, then counting the spoons one more time before rolling them into the towel—and she took them home herself.

In the bus after school, my neighbor told me her allowance was five dollars a week, which she saved up in the ceramic piggy bank on top of her dresser. Her godmother took her shopping in the city twice a year so she could buy birthday and Christmas presents for her family.

On top of her pretty bookshelf sat a crystal vase. Under it, on the first shelf, she kept her diary—which she did not write in— with its beautiful gold key. Next to that was an oversized dictionary, which she was not allowed to open until she was in college. On the lower shelves stood the unopened leather-bound volumes of my dreams: Encyclopedia Britannica.

She never did order a single book from Scholastic and wouldn't borrow one of mine when I offered. Maybe she was afraid she might wrinkle a page by mistake.

Frank Sinatra Had That Twist of a Smile

My mom and her best friend, like all teenage girls, wore bobby socks and tight white sweaters buttoned up over practical cotton bras that crinkled flat unless stuffed with toilet paper, a commodity scarce in my grandmother's house.

Frankie smoked on the steps behind the theatre. The cigarette-less girls hovered, breathless. They silently dreamed of coyly asking for a light, while keeping their virgin breath kissable sweet.

Frankie took one last drag, flicked the white stick with the glowing red tip from his lips, stamped it out on the sidewalk, and turned on his heel.

No sooner had his toe lifted from the pavement, than the two girls collided, converging on the smoldering carcass of molten dreams.

Triumphant, my mom held the still fiercely-hot butt aloft, just out of reach of her petite pal, her compadre in the war between the sexes.

The look of disgust curled Frankie's lip!

"Girls, you don't want *that*."

But, Frankie would offer them nothing else.

They couldn't ask him for what they could only imagine might be on their periphery. It was nothing they could visualize, much less articulate.

Genuflection

It had been a sin for Catholics to step inside a church that wasn't Catholic. But when they changed that rule, the following week our public school took a class trip to the town's large Methodist church to join up with all the local schools to sing a song about world peace.

One of my Catholic friends walked up the aisle just ahead of me. But, when we got near the front of the church and prepared to enter the pew and sit with our classmates, she realized that, before entering the pew in the Catholic church, it was a requirement to genuflect at the altar, on which sat the chalice holding the hosts. Consecrated hosts held the physical incarnation of God.

No one in this church was genuflecting.

My friend was terribly upset that she might sin, not knowing whether, in this church, God was present at the altar and would require her genuflection; or whether it was as true this week, as the week before, that the people in this church were all heathens, doomed to hell, and she would be committing a mortal sin if she genuflected to an altar empty of the true presence of God.

In a panic, she asked me, a fellow Catholic, what we should do.

My fifth-grade self realized my friend would pee her pants if I did not make up a good story—and fast.

I told her to genuflect in front of the altar, as she would have done at St. Joseph's. But, in her mind, she should genuflect, not to the marble altar, but to God Himself, who, like Schrödinger's Cat, might be, or might not be, present and alive in the hosts on the altar. From where we stood in line, we could not see whether there was even a chalice, and we had no idea whether there were any hosts in this kind of a church, or whether a Methodist priest could even consecrate a host to transform it into the corporeal presence of God, or if a Catholic priest had made a special trip here in advance of our arrival, just to consecrate the hosts, to make sure everything was done properly according to Catholic protocol, given that the pope had given his blessing and permission that we could be here at all.

Genuflect, I told her, just as if this were a Catholic church. I reasoned that it was necessary to genuflect, just in case God was present at this altar—it would be a grievous sin not to.

But, as everyone knows, God is everywhere, even in this church, even among heathens. Just tell God, in your heart—God, wherever You are, this genuflection is for You.

I told her, we are human, and fallible, but God is love and God is forgiving. If it is a mistake to genuflect in a heathen church at a heathen altar, tell the priest at confession, and you will be forgiven. But, either way, if you genuflect, God will know what is in your heart.

Though no one else genuflected, but filed into the pews in an orderly fashion and without hesitation, we both genuflected and crossed ourselves.

No one else seemed to notice or care what we did.

Haunting Refrain

My mother does not play piano anymore, but keeps her mother's piano in the living room, where my sister sits on it, in an urn.

It's not really my sister, it's her ashes.

My sister always said, "When I die, I want my ashes strewn from the observation deck at the tippity-top of Sunrise Mountain, the most beautiful place on the planet!"

My mother wishes to keep her daughter's ashes on her mother's piano, and wishes to keep her mother's piano in her living room with the cover over the keys, since nobody plays anymore.

"I'm not ready to let her go," says my mother, when I beg her to let me strew my sister's ashes. My sister dragged visitors from all the ends of the earth to Sunrise Mountain. To gaze out over paradise. To soak in the love of the universe.

I want to lead my mother by the hand and get her singing "Shower the People" by James Taylor and have her sway and wave her arms overhead and watch the sunrise and watch the sunset and remember how wonderful it was to share the planet with someone so alive.

Silent now, the piano, my sister, my mother, my father, and me. We sit in my mother's living room and quietly assemble the jigsaw puzzle of Mount Everest.

Haze

While I was on a band trip visiting a high school in a small town in Montreal, I ran out of Marlboro Lights and discovered Canadian cigarettes. I liked the smooth sound of the French name, "du Maurier." The clerk at the mom-and-pop store assured me in a gorgeously French accent that the fine print on the label translated to "easier on the throat."

My quitting of my nicotine addiction was still several months off, but, like high-school graduation, I sensed it looming on the horizon, an iceberg silently sneaking its way toward the Titanic. I hated smoking, the taste and smell of cigarettes, and my lungs hurt when I ran during gym class. I had always been one of the "good kids." Good kids weren't supposed to smoke, but we'd all tried it. I blushed at the memory of where I was and who I was with when I lit up my first wicked stick.

From then on, I had been a closet smoker. Literally— smoking in my bedroom closet. I naïvely had no idea the smell of smoke lingers, and the only reason I hadn't been caught is my parents were too busy to notice. They had full-time jobs, PTA, and bridge parties. What with fixing the roof and mowing the lawn and keeping track of my seven younger brothers and sisters, they trusted me not to give them any trouble.

The two bands practiced that afternoon in the school's auditorium. We Americans sat side by side with the kids with the funny accents. When we took a break, we were told to hang out and get to know each other until they called us for dinner. We all tried to squeeze into the tiny band room, but I had not been able to find my flute case, so I waited in the hall, carrying my flute with me so I wouldn't lose it.

I looked for a place to stand where no one would notice me. I sidled up next to a boy who was standing by himself leaning against the wall across from the band room door.

I recognized him. Though he was often absent, skipping school, he was the best player in our school's saxophone section.

I knew he was a loner, and I was pretty sure he would not be attempting to engage me in pleasant conversation. I hoped he might not mind me standing there, and hoped he would just ignore me as I hoped to be able to simply ignore him.

My plan worked. We stood in the hall in silence. No one noticed us. I was hungry, but, just like at home, I had to wait until the powers that be authorized the clanging of the dinner bell.

We did not speak. He might have been a statue. I hoped he had his eyes shut, behind his sunglasses, and did not notice me staring. During rehearsals back home, I often found myself gazing at his unkempt, ravishing curls and wondering about his no-smile lips. He did not wear clothes typical of the jocks or the geeks, but neither did he wear the bell-bottomed jeans and tie-dyed shirts of the druggies. Just a well-worn, faded cotton shirt and ill-fitting, bland gray pants without creases or a belt. Probably hand-me-downs. He generally looked like he had just fallen out of bed wearing the same wrinkled clothes he had fallen asleep in the night before. Mirrors, if they even existed in his house, did not warrant his reflection.

I had long admired his sax playing. Unlike me, he had mastered the art of improvisation and needed no sheet music. I'd often stayed after school an extra hour just to hear him wax eloquent on his instrument. His unusual music filled the recesses of my brain, flowed through my entire being, and turned me to water.

The band room became louder and raucous. Without a lookout in the crow's nest to keep a watchful eye, students edged out into the hall, pushing and laughing and teasing.

The boy I was standing next to was leaning against the wall, but started surreptitiously sliding along the wall away from me, as if trying to sneak down the hall and get away from the larger group of students without being noticed. I was eager for any excuse to avoid being caught up in the chatty chaos of my classmates, so I followed him, step for step. Each time he edged a little further down the hall and away from me, I edged up nearer him and closed the wider gap between us.

He noticed what I was doing, and I noticed him, noticing me. Inexplicably, we both started giggling. I knew we were breaking the rules, venturing way out beyond the limits demanded by crowd control, down the hallway, farther and farther away from where we had been instructed to remain. I thought it was funny, our futile little struggle against the conformity required of us as students. Back in our home town, I usually felt anchored at school, as if invisibly tethered to someplace not exactly specified, under house arrest, not free to go, held for an indeterminate period of time. Here in this foreign school, no teacher seemed in charge of monitoring the hall. There were no obvious chaperones. No one in authority noticed the ranks were breaking up. Most of the students were accidental rebels, pushed along by the crowd, much as dead fish are washed up higher and higher on the beach as the tide rolls in.

Scooting down the hall ahead of our classmates, this boy and I were taking it a little farther than the rest. The two of us were soon edging down the hallway faster and faster. We reached the end of the corridor, where there was a huge, handwritten sign, "No Exit," attached to the back of a chair. It was meant to block our passage, to let us know we had reached the perimeter of the area within which students were allowed to wander. We were teetering on the edge of the space to which we visitors had been invited, and at the legal limits. Our exploration of the strange school should be at an end. But, around the corner, the next hallway loomed. The ceiling lights there, where we were not allowed, were dimmed.

The boy peeked around me and, looking back over my shoulder to see if anyone behind me was paying any attention to him, he gave a few, furtive, sidelong glances toward the far end of the hall. Seeing the coast was clear, he turned once to look me in the eye, gave a quick nod of his head, then took off in the direction of the darkness.

Was he meaning for me to follow him? I watched him disappear around the corner, then I ran to catch up. He glided along the tiled floor purposefully, brazenly striding into the restricted area as if he were on a mission. I was entranced by the intrigue. As if he were the White Rabbit and I, Alice, I followed.

We had escaped our detention. Once free, we ran.

I started laughing, a little hysterically, if, from nothing else, then from the fright of not knowing why it was I was not behaving myself. It was totally out of character. I had never before caught myself being this naughty. I was always reliable. I always stayed exactly where I knew I was supposed to be. I had made it almost through my senior year without ever getting into trouble.

I did not want to be caught, and I ran faster. Soon, we were in a race. We quashed our giggles as we hurried the length of the hallway without a destination. We didn't know where we were, nor whether any of the offices were occupied with people conducting meetings or other school business after hours.

We turned the next corner into even stranger territory. The wall was lined with glass cases, sports trophies and plaques announcing years of championships. At the end of the hall, the glow of streetlights streamed in through the large windows. We had reached the main entrance to the school. We slowed to a stop under the "Exit" sign.

The boy, whose name I did not know, began slowly retracing his steps, retreating from the front door, returning into the darkness. He was feeling the walls with his hands. Going backwards, he passed me, heading in the direction from which we had come. He lit a match and held it up to read the labels on the wall next to each heavy wooden door. When he found the one labeled "Principal," I watched breathlessly as he picked the lock.

I now stood rock still, sincerely worried. How and why had this kid learned the skill of lock-picking? I wondered about his family, and I guessed they were not at all like mine.

He opened the door, pushed me inside, and locked the door behind us.

I was shocked. But, still, I was not too worried. He was smaller than me, and I was pretty strong, for a girl. Stronger than most boys. I didn't think he could overpower me. Still, I was confused by his behavior.

And, by mine. I had never done anything this crazy in my life. Break into the principal's office? It was absurd. It was exhilarating, scary, and fun. But really scary.

The boy handed me a book of matches and whispered for me to light one. Seeing no reason not to, aside from the possibility of a random, fatal fire that would burn down the school and kill us all, I cooperated.

I began to worry. Was he a firebug? Or, one of those crazies, who might actually have had a gun and a plan?

I held up the lit matches, one by one, so he could see by the flickering light while he ransacked the principal's desk drawers. He swore under his breath as he came up empty, over and over.

Then he turned to the bookcase, and he found what he had been looking for—the stash where the principal hid his liquor. He took a swig, which I assumed must have been whiskey, for it was the only alcoholic beverage I had ever seen anyone drink that was from a large glass bottle. I had led a very sheltered life, and I rarely paid attention to what other people did if it didn't immediately pertain to me, but I had seen my uncle pour shots of whiskey after dinner, one for my Irish grandfather and one for himself.

The sax player drank fairly quickly, and it seemed he was trying to drink as much as possible, as though he could ignore what must have been the burning in his throat. I had never seen anyone drunk. I wondered whether I should start to be even more worried.

The boy then proceeded to take a Manila file folder out of a drawer and empty its contents onto the desk. He folded the Manila paper into what I soon realized was a sturdy makeshift ashtray. Another handy skill he had had to have learned from a mentor in the dark arts.

He lit a cigarette, took a drag, and handed it to me. He lit another and, after a few drags, propped it into the crease of his "ashtray" and picked up his sax. He was not planning to burn down the school, after all. I was relieved.

I smoked in the dark. His cigarettes were a cheap American brand, not as smooth as du Maurier's. I felt like choking.

I realized I was sitting in the chair reserved for unhappy visitors to the Principal's Office, where the principal, seated in his comfortable leathered armchair, could scold them from the other side of the desk.

I very curious about this boy, and started wondering about his life of desperation, one in which he needed to know both the art of lock-picking and how to find his way into a stranger's liquor, but I dared not open my mouth to ask my questions.

Such nerve—the Principal's Office! He knew no fear of authority. Or, he was super-practiced at not getting caught. On the latter possibility, I pinned my hopes of getting into a good college with my reputation still intact.

He started playing, drifting in on the bell of his sax, imperceptibly at first, into the thin air and without waiting for a cue. Quietly crooning to no one but the silver emptiness of silence, his instrument was praying to a god I suspected the musician knew could not exist.

He pressed on, as though sailing through the frost of a late December in an empty sleigh, the one in which Santa was supposed to ride. But Santa had never shown up with the bag of toys the other kids depended on to lighten the season of their longest nights.

He leaned his head into the music, pressing against the breast of the new moon, nuzzling the stuffed bear his aunt had given him at his last birthday party, the one when she had suddenly keeled over, having had a stroke, and died. The one family event that lingers in his memory as his last party, the one when he turned four. The teddy bear, ever since, missing.

He groaned into his horn, made his fearless, insistent sounds through the insatiable chill of darkness.

As if I wasn't there.

Blues or jazz, I didn't know the difference, but I did appreciate that it was not our marching band music and he did not play from memory. His mouthpiece slid effortlessly between his lips, the reed eased along by the yellow slime coating his unbrushed, nicotine-stained teeth.

He held the vibrating reed in the center of a muscular mouth which appeared to have been daily exercised for this very purpose. His lips and teeth parted intermittently, only long enough to allow in the next bellowful of air. Then the tendons in his neck strained and he again reached with his head to grasp for the musical tool. It was alive with a dance of its own.

His soulful notes came from stored, pent-up grit, which he let loose, slowly at first, in a measured majesty befitting a tribute to the gods. Playing quietly, he offered appeasement to those he would not wish to risk offending, who might unleash their terrible power, should they find displeasure with his performance. Mars,

God of War. Thor, God of Thunder. Odin, Neptune, Zeus, and every other deity sat quietly in their seats in the balcony, enraptured by his song, but poised and ready to rend the Earth at any moment with lightning bolts, cracking whips of thunder, spurting lava, eager to blow apart mountain tops and rip out a typhoon to decimate the islands. Creators of this universe and judges of its human inhabitants, they stood upright in the open cart of the heavenly chariot, waiting to slap the reins to guide the stallions to stampede. They'd be thrilled to see dashing hoofbeats leave risen faults of earthquakes in their path.

But the gods, mesmerized by the soul of the sax, moved not a muscle.

My admiration for this young kid's guts in this whole matter overfilled my heart. He made it up, this continuous outpouring, as he proceeded to play, pausing only for breath when his lungs were completely emptied, then gulping in reinforcements for another round of ecstasy. He cried into his reed with a despair as if they were one body, he and and his sax, devoted lovers, and with an urgency as if, inexplicably, his mouthpiece was suddenly resisting his advances.

Through his music, the morning dove cried its eternal loneliness, the swan whose mate never made it back to the pond wailed its lost heart, my hours in front of the bathroom mirror, spent in despair of ever seeing my breasts grow large enough to attract a member of the opposite sex, screamed back at me from the bell at the end of the hollow tube where his fingers danced.

I longed to riffle his touseled hair with my own free-wandering fingers. His never-smile lips held me fast, in silent awe of his control over every muscle in his body. I was sure Death himself admired the way this young man could remain still for eternity.

And his music. His soul-scraping music.

As he played this love song, I smoked and smoked, trying to make myself less invisible, hoping to shine silver-gray in the darkness. But he never once stopped and tried to kiss me, no matter how I twirled the slender, white paper enfolding the tobacco between my fingers, sexy as Jean Harlow or any other silver-screen siren. And no matter how the curling haze rose around my head and encircled my long, straight blonde hair, defining me as one of "those" girls, he did not notice.

Smoke got to my eyes and stuck to my blue mascara-clotted, batting eyelashes. I felt the stabbing in my severely irritated corneas, the watering in my eyes filling me with a new urgency to quit the habit once and for all.

Though I knew he could not see me in the haze, which merely blended in with the night darkness all around me, I never gave up—I blew elegant smooth streams of come-hither smoky bliss through pursed lips, hoping he had seen those movies and lusted for Jean Harlow. I created beautiful wisps to silhouette my face, which was lit only by the glowing ember end of the cigarette.

He and I were on separate planets. On his, he encountered only his reed, which trembled in vibration at the caress by his mouth. It whispered its adoration, in hushed tones calling him by his name: Lord, the Powerful, the Divine.

I smoked so much I started coughing. I had to put down the cigarette and raise my elbows to my chin. I held both hands over my mouth, hoping to stifle the gutteral sputtering. Anyone walking by in the hall could hear, and I fervently hoped no one would bust us before my musician was ready to end our private jam session.

The hall remained vacant of familiar noise.

I managed to regain my composure, but dared not even think of speaking, sure I would burst out in a coughing fit that might require medical attention.

We had been gone from our appointed station for approximately fifteen years—or was it twenty minutes?

He pulled his reed from his mouth.

"Don't you want to play your flute?

"No, I don't have my music—"

I realized how lame that must have sounded as soon as the words escaped my lips. Blast the blasphemy of needing sheet music! My dreams of being soulmate to a musician were dashed. I could never again look at him expecting there would ever be anything more between us than what we'd just shared.

And I was the only one who'd shared anything at all that glimmered with hopes for a lasting intimacy, and he had no way of knowing that, unless he had been able to read my mind. He had never given me the slightest indication that a connection with him would ever be more than ephemeral, ever more than a nod in passing on the way to our seats in the band room or onto the high school concert stage.

The mist of the after-rain dissipated quickly. The full storm never had the chance to envelop the sky, never hinted at the possibility of waiting for the sun or the expectation of a rainbow.

And, quickly as that, it was over.

I could see by the slight rise of his blond-bearded chin he had calculated it was too dangerous to stay where we were any longer. I was sure someone must have already noticed we were missing, and expected that at any moment they would come looking, turn on the lights outside in the hallway, turn the key in the lock, and stride in through the opened door, holding, balanced in the crook of an elbow, a clipboard and a pen, the disciplinarian poised mid-air to take down both our names.

I had to give up my fantasy about having my first sleepover with a boy in a room full of dictionaries, Manila files with reports on bad kids, and liquor bottles. As he calmly packed up to go, I said goodbye to the oaken swivel chairs and an outdated globe that showed the world as it used to be.

In his own time, my officemate took a final swig of the liquor, gathered up his cigarettes and sax, and unlocked the door. We left it closed and ran back down the hall, playing cowboys and Indians all the way, pretend-shooting each other with our memories of childhood bows and arrows and six-shooters. We hammed it up, silently war-hooping and gun-slinging, getting shot and writhing in dramatic ecstasy as we fell to the floor to die after a proper amount of tortured wriggling. We jumped to our feet before every corner to peek that no one was there to see us.

I wondered if we would be caught after the fact, smoke on our breath. More likely, the ashes on the principal's desk would be discovered only by the janitor, much later, and our dastardly deed left unreported, totted up to "those damned kids," who were not worth the effort it would take to write up the incident.

Would no one but me remember this night?

On the long bus ride back to New Jersey, the sax player slept stretched out in a three-seater while I chain-smoked du Maurier's across the aisle in a seat all by myself. I faced the window, coughing and sputtering and swearing under what was left of my breath.

Silently fuming. I was sure Jean Harlow would never have been left unkissed.

He Came Out of Nowhere

He was dancing on toe like Muhammad Ali, jabbing straight ahead at my knees with his tiny little fists, circling me like a pack of hyenas.

But, there was just him.

Who was this little stranger, beating my legs to a pulp? I had no enemies I knew of. Most certainly, none who were no older than six.

He was cursing and punching and kicking me incessantly.

Could it be my fate, I was Customer Service at the center of his universe, and he was demanding a refund?

It was the first day of school after summer vacation. I was juggling a huge pile of textbooks and a flute case. Though I twisted my neck and strained to look down, I could not see his face.

Two blocks more, uphill from the bus stop, and I'd be home.

He dogged me almost all the way, leaving off only when he turned off the street and, heaving great sobs, raced up a driveway. He disappeared inside the one house I'd never entered, two doors down from my own. That falling down hovel, where the two teenaged bullies lived.

He never even closed the front door.

Hold-Me-Tight

My uncle would say, "Mama, that's a Hold-Me-Tight," as he served my grandmother a sandwich which required two hands to not fall apart.

Her gnarled fingers would explore the plate she couldn't see, first discovering the curve of the rim, the edge of the delicate ceramic centered on the dining table in front of her wheelchair.

She'd lean in a bit, her expressionless face never changing, even as her fingers drawled from the smooth edge toward the plate's center, bumped into the crusts, scooped under and lifted the bread, and pushed the slices and their contents together.

She did not know if she held Virginia ham and Swiss with sliced onion, lettuce, and mustard on pumpernickel; or tuna salad made with celery and sliced green grapes, with a slice each of cucumber and beefsteak tomato, on whole wheat; or American cheese and alfalfa sprouts on white with mayo; or a BLT on toasted rye.

My uncle never said.

She only knew it was not peanut butter and jelly, which, even she could see, was the only sandwich that would hold together on its own, whether you held it tight, or not.

I Can See

My neighbor is visibly distressed. His left eye has decided it will no longer cooperate. It had reported to his brain that the world had disappeared. It could not know about the clot, the bit of blood gone AWOL, blocking the light.

It's only an eye.

Even as my neighbor insisted that the world is intact, his left eye continued to report to his brain that it saw no evidence to support the fact.

My neighbor believes his left eye has become a scoundrel. He rants on about his left eye, decrying its treachery, its disavowal of their long-standing mutual respect. It's as if my neighbor's left eye has never done a thing in its life but to give my neighbor grief.

I listen in sympathy.

My neighbor conspires with the doctor in torturing his left eye, to attempt to force it to resume doing its job.

His left eye dutifully reports its pain, but keeps insisting it tells the truth. No matter how many jabs with hypodermic needles, scalpel incisions, or suction treatments, it will not crumble under pressure. It swears it is doing its very best, as it always has done, and pleads its case. Its loyalty to the body has never wavered.

It is the world that has changed, and not me! says my neighbor's left eye.

My neighbor's right eye begs to differ. It sends its own report directly to my neighbor's brain.

The world is right there! Plain as the small, black mole on my neighbor's cheek.

My neighbor weeps at the obvious betrayal by his long-time trusted companion and helpmeet, his left eye. His left eye has no shame, will not admit its sin.

The eye that is not right, weeps. It cannot convincingly convey what it sees, in any other way. It despairs of finding a witness to verify what can only be a bitter truth—one which my neighbor refuses to acknowledge—the world is gone.

I Got Out of Bed Today

Today, I got out of bed. But, I define "today" quite loosely—the hours my eyes are open. I never check the clock anymore. Or the calendar.

And I guess it does count as "out of bed," even if it was only two quick trips to the bathroom. And even if I did rush back under the covers. It was a "sauntering" rush, not a "rushed" rush.

I'm thankful for yesterday. I remembered to refill my water glass, since I'd spilled some. And I put two apples on the nightstand, Yellow Delicious. I found the book I wanted to reread, *Pride and Prejudice,* and put it on the little table next to the nightstand, along with a couple of bags of potato chips. Well, actually, a lot of potato chips. The bags are labeled "Party Size," and each has twelve little bags of potato chips in it. I love potato chips. I still have three little bags left.

I also added a bar of dark chocolate with salted caramel bits to the food stash in my bedroom, which I like to keep stocked up in case of emergency. And I did have some more fruit, if you count jelly-donut jelly as a fruit—and what else would it be? I do eat plenty of fruits and vegetables, mostly at restaurant salad bars.

And I got a box of Saltines from the pantry. I'd almost run out.

Today, I don't need to shower or change clothes. I'm still clean from yesterday. And besides, Americans waste too much water and pollute the environment with too many cleaning products.

I've been getting a lot done. I've been practicing my strong points—procrastination, timing, and changing my mind. I read all the time. Labels. And, I exercise.

Well, at least my thumbs. I try not to take myself too seriously. I try to relax and let go. I write a lot of poetry on my phone, and I find it's getting easier to let go of grammar and punctuation. I'm getting better at it.

I got out of bed today as much as I want to. I'm good.

I Made My Own Music

This was a year I spent in quietude, reflection, introspection, and deep mourning. I did not wear black, did not scream to the gods of their errors in judgment in having taken the wrong two people, emptying the crooks of both my elbows.

Aghast at the vast looming, all around, the terror of the red night, the sour of the frothing seas, and the slime and stench of man-made cesspools, I stood apart and wondered what next to do with my life.

I took time off from the making of that decision and marked time in the hollow of the arts. I studied freely—art, history, and poetry—and relished the hard work and the feeling of being enlarged by success. I wove consolation for my orphandom by continuation of old friendships, though I had my doubts that my ability to be fervent, to *be there* for a friend in our moments together, ever would have survived this unexpected rending of my own heart.

I still dwelt in the abyss of my loss.

I indulged, finally, in conversation, and found, to my relief and enjoyment, I could do so guiltlessly. For the first time, my words would not circle their way back to my mother's ear and fly back out at me on her disparaging tongue.

I had a decision to make. Life is too short to mourn forever.

Or, it is not, and there is nothing left to do, but to mourn.

I killed myself in droves of absences, neglected my children, my health, my husband, my clock. I gingerly gave up singing in my favorite choir. I mourned the drenching of my voice.

But, yesterday, I discovered these past few months of deliberate non-attendance at the sun's dancing party has indeed been long enough to drown out chaotic echoes of admiration, approbation, and applause, my mother's way of draping me, cocooning me, entombing me so she could keep me safe; me, her "mother's child," sure to be still alive so long as she was wrapped in her mother's protective embrace.

Surprising me, as I was driving home, alone on the road, I heard my father's voice.

At first, it merely stumbled, climbing its way up from my gut. Then, its roaring engulfed my car in flames.

The soothing scratch for itch was making its escape.

> *What do you do with a drunken sailor?*
> *What do you do with a drunken sailor?*
> *What do you do with a drunken sailor?*
> *Earl! Lie! In! The! More! Nin!*

I heard the boom of my father's tenor pouring from my own throat.

> *Put him in the scuppers and wet him all over!*

Dad first took up the accoustic guitar when he was in the army and lonely, away from home for the first time in his life. He accompanied himself as he sang folksongs, the same songs his father sang to him when he was a child, the same songs he sang to me and my siblings . . . .

. . . .

Excuse me a moment. I have to go and get out my guitar.

. . . .

I have got to learn to play this thing.

I Never Said Goodbye to My Kindergarten Teacher

Just the thought of my red scarf—the one I left at school on purpose, knowing it would be gone for good—and my cheeks grow hot with shame and my heart's blood runs cold with guilt. At the end of the kindergarten day, we had to get our stuff from the coat rack and the cubbies. But I never recognized the scarf as mine, though it was soft, and beautiful, and I loved it. I just never found mine missing.

Not until I was cold. Then, I would remember where it was. At the bus stop, if it was sunny, I felt warmth on my face. Yet, winter's promise of snow lingered, and dipping my un-legginged knees into the icy air called into focus the place my scarf slept. I vowed each morning, I'd wear it home that night.

Shivering on the playground, I could trace the scarf, in my mind, to its hook in the row of hooks. But on mild winter days, the wind didn't blow, the frost didn't cross the street—it withheld its insistent, stiff embrace. I forgot I owned a crimson, knitted warmer.

Spring finally melted trees. Snow banks were mown of their ice-cold threads. Bushes glowed with new leaves. Life was all running creeks, dances through April puddles, budding dandelions, a warm breeze. I forgot about red scarves and cold thighs and knees.

Until, that hot day at the end of June, my kindly teacher tenderly waved the class goodbye, my good, red scarf in her hand. That last day, I listened; so familiar was the tune, I sang along. As the teacher held it up and waved the flag over her head, we all crooned, "Somebody's mother is going to be mad. They left their good, red scarf at school!"

And I heard the echo of my own mother's voice—how many times—"Whatever happened to your good, red scarf? I know you took it to school!"

She had asked me, week after week; I didn't know where it hid.

Here in plain sight.

I lowered my eyes, in agony. I knew my limits. I was not going to be able to 'fess up without bursting into an endless, heart-wrenching, soul-wracking, gut-busting, blubbering sob-fest—I shied from the impending disaster and stoically lowered myself in my seat, hoping my scarlet complexion wouldn't give me away.

My cheeks burned in humiliation. I choked down voiceless confessions, the loss already suffered.

It had been a gift from Santa.

And I hoped no one noticed the deliberate scarf-losing guilt crossing my determined, wretched face.

I Shouldn't Have Married a Believer

My husband bakes bread for fun, using up our yeast during the pandemic, when store shelves are already empty and there's no yeast in the pipeline.

He plans to go to the store tomorrow, believing there is always more yeast, more in the store of whatever it is you need. It's on the shelf, or at least they have some in the back. It's always there, waiting for you, for whenever you decide you need it. Just ask somebody.

My husband's never gone to the store and not found everything he desires, right there on the shelf, waiting for him to buy it.

I tell him a story. There was a time during a crisis when there was no more oil to be had in the store, and it took a miracle of God to make the oil stores last.

He says, people must have had oil stashed away. They were probably selfishly saving it for their own emergencies and wouldn't share.

I tell him the story of the time there was plenty of yeast, but no time to wait for bread to rise, and the people baked their bread unleavened and called it matzo, and, since we're out of bread and we're out of yeast, but we have flour, I'll make matzo today.

He can't imagine why I would want to make matzo when we like bread better, and there's always enough time for bread to rise, and he's going shopping tomorrow for toilet paper and can pick up some yeast.

I've Got to Care More

Really, I don't know when my aunt's next-door neighbor's nephew's goddaughter's birthday is.

And I've openly said, "I don't care what your co-worker's wife's cousin's twins managed to do. Yes, it's sad that they're challenged. They need extra help. But, they're only conjoined at the head."

I was shocked—I was the first to have told my twenty-two-year-old visitor that yes, I know that you do have one leg six inches shorter due to a childhood illness, and yes, it must be difficult to hit the center of the bowl, and yes, it is difficult to get down to the floor to wipe up pee, but you *can* leave the bathroom clean when you're done.

And, he did.

And, he was grateful for the new information, that he was an adult human being perfectly capable of being responsible for physically taking care of himself.

And he was able to do it, just fine. But, from the time he was seven years old and had suffered his illness, he'd been told that it was okay that he was helpless. He was seen as an incompetent invalid, and told that only a monster wouldn't pity him and willingly clean up after him.

And, they'd said, any compassionate person would do anything for him without a word of complaint or question, so as not to cause him to lose face.

Learning To Play Blades of Grass

My friend next door taught me the melodies of the forest. I knew how babies, abandoned in their cribs, struggled in terrified anguish as Mother cooked or cleaned and did other, ambiguous, mother-things and had to ignore the babies' "crocodile tears" so she could get things done.

I relentlessly beat at the clouds, the fence protecting God and his angels from raw awareness of the babies' plight. My blades of grass were roaring, thunderous, monstrous beasts, calling for divine assistance.

A fresh blade of grass will screech loudly when you hold it right and blow on it. Pluck a blade of grass longer than your thumb. Keep it straight and be careful not to wrinkle it. You will be folding your hands into prayer, then holding the blade taut between your two thumbs, adjacent and pressing, wall to wall, and creating a space on either side of the taut blade. When you purse your lips and blow across the blade of grass, blow hard into the space between your thumbs, and the blade will vibrate and make a loud screeching noise.

Here is how you will position your hands: Hold your empty hands in front of you, palms facing each other. Spread your fingers. Curl your fingers down onto your palms to make two tight fists. Keep your thumbs to the outside of your fists. Point your thumbs straight up. Bring your two fists together, pressing tightly with the knuckles of your fingers and the bottoms of your palms. Press your upright-pointing thumbs together, side by side at the knuckles. Roll the bottom two knuckles of each thumb outward to create a small space between the top and bottom knuckles. That space is where you will blow into with pursed lips, once you have positioned the blade of grass there properly. The blade will be straight up and down, stretched taut, and held tight in two places, at the top and bottom of the thumbs, above and below the empty space.

Here is how to position the blade to make it taut between the thumbs. As you work at positioning the blade, you must work at always returning the hands to formation during and after every step. Pick up the blade of grass and hold it straight up longwise. Turn the blade sideways so one long skinny edge is facing your lips. Position the blade, upright longwise, stretched between the top and the bottom of your two thumbs, pressed tight between the two knuckles at the top and pressed tight between the two knuckles at the bottom. Now, work at pulling the blade as straight and long as possible, so it is taut between the knuckles of your thumbs. Using one index finger, hold the bottom of the blade in place. Press the blade tightly between the two thumbs' lower knuckles to secure it in place, then release the finger. Using the other index finger and top of the thumb on its hand, grasp the top of the blade and pull it straight up into position. Press the blade tightly between the two thumbs' top knuckles, to secure it in place, then release the finger. Adjust the blade, over and over, until it is laying flat, taut between your tightly-pressed-together thumbs. When the blade is stretched taut, pressed tightly between your thumbs, roll the thumb knuckles outward a bit until there is a bit of empty space on either side of the blade. Through pursed lips, blow air straight at the blade, making sure not to touch the blade with your lips.

The lips do not produce any sound at all, they just blow air. It is the vibrating of the taut blade that produces the screech. Even if the blade is positioned correctly and you are blowing in the right spot, it might take a bit of practice to get the blade to vibrate. Blowing too little air will produce no vibration. Blowing too much air will stiffen the blade and eliminate the sound. Adjust the tautness of the blade and the size of the empty space to raise or lower the pitch and the volume of the sound. A looser blade will produce a lower-pitched sound. If it is too loose, it will not vibrate at all. If the blade is too taut, there will be no room for it to vibrate.

With practice, a combination of adjustments to the positioning of the lips and thumbs and to the volume of air blown will allow control over a range of pitches and volumes.

Live-Streaming 2020: The COVID Test

As instructed, I pull into a parking space next to the picnic tables at the side of the Medical Arts building, roll down my window, and wait in my car for my COVID test. Before I can pick up my phone to call the office to let them know I've arrived, I see, on the other side of the car parked next to mine, a nurse is placing a long white swab into a test tube.

It really *is* long, I realize, silently wondering how far up she will be able to go into my own sinuses before striking my brain or poking a nerve in such a way as the nerves in my delicate nasal passages have specifically instructed me they decline to be poked.

The nurse sees me staring at her in anticipation of the horror I'm sure is awaiting me, and asks me if I'm here for a COVID test. I answer her through my Halloween pandemic mask, the one I'm still using, though Halloween is over. It's my mask of choice whenever I have to go out into the world with its cooties. The white cotton fabric is decorated with a melange of grinning Jack-O-Lanterns, ghosts, bats, skeletons, and witch's cauldrons, properly conducive to conveying the message that my mask conceals facial expressions of childish delight at encounters with the macabre.

"Yes," I say, and I give the nurse my name before she asks.

"Stay here," she says, "I'll bring your test out." She goes into the building through the side door. I breathe a tiny sigh of relief that she did not happen to have a test for me already conveniently on her, tucked into a pocket of her blue scrubs—a waitress at Yetter's Diner will have extra straws in the apron of her uniform, ready to pull out on demand, and peel off the paper wrapper and shove it brusquely into the surface of your glass of Coke between the ice cubes, floating in the foam like mini icebergs looking for their Titanic—and immediately jab it deep into the recesses of my skull without warning.

Tense as an angler's line fighting its marlin, I had been ready for her, just in case. As I watched her stride through the parking lot, I judged the distance to where I guessed my own COVID test kit waited. As I have an appointment, my name must already be written in black magic marker on a label, which she would peel off and wrap around the test tube after putting my swab in it, as she had done with the sample from her previous victim … er, I mean, patient … the woman who I had seen in the car next to mine when I'd arrived.

I presumed the whole testing procedure was likely streamlined, as an assembly line, the row of kits and labels neatly lined up on a table temporarily set up in the hallway outside the doctor's office, conveniently near the building's emergency exit, now put to new use during the pandemic.

This nurse must spend all day on her feet, repeating this one task. I wonder if she misses the variety of patients she normally sees when there's nothing unusual afoot: tonsillectomies, hernias, and other operations people now put off due to fear of the virus. This COVID-testing circus has only one pony. I calculate that it should take the nurse at least two minutes to get back inside the building, check off my name from her list, pick up a test to use on me, and walk back to my car.

I apologize in advance to the nerve endings far up inside my respiratory passageway. I wonder if it is too late to practice preventative methods for heading off pain. Transcendental meditation, mindfulness, reiki, Lamaze: I wonder which would be most efficacious in distracting me from awareness of what is about to happen within my own body.

I look at my reflection in the side view mirror of my car. I see the terrified look on my face, and feel sorry for myself. So, it's come to this, I think. I have 2020 to thank for the fact that I've willingly driven myself to meet up with a medieval torturer. I have less than two minutes to decide to chicken out, put my car into drive, and skedaddle out of there, quick, before the nurse gets back.

I'm already planning my escape route. I'll pull over at the Quick Chek gas station and call the doctor's office from my cell phone.

What would sound least implausible?

I decide on "I felt nauseous, and I think I have food poisoning, so I had to leave. I'll call to reschedule when I've recovered. I think it was the potato salad at the barbecue yesterday." I realize I would immediately be found out a liar. No one is going to barbecues in November, especially not during a pandemic.

On second thought, since there's no indoor restaurant dining now, due to the pandemic, and no indoor visiting with friends and families, people might be feeling crazy enough to picnic outside in forty-two-degree weather.

I recalled now, how, as the car next to mine pulled out of its parking space and turned, then passed in front of mine, I could see the driver through my windshield. As she headed for the exit from the parking lot, she was rubbing her face alongside of her nose. I saw she was crying.

My imagination ran away with me. I projected onto her all my fear, my worry over the possibilty of experiencing my own major discomfort—no, agony!—which I was anticipating would be awful to the point of being unbearably excruciating.

With no evidence, I leapt to certitude. The woman had been crying in reaction to intense pain, both pointed and, by now, throbbing. Pain, caused by a relentless probing of her nasal cavity by the nurse, digging through the rubble of Pompeii, searching for victims ... er, I mean, viruses ...

I tried to calm myself down, to think more ... more reasonably. It was possible the middle-aged woman in her car had merely been listening to a sad song on the radio. Maybe the break-up song from high school from when her first boyfriend had dumped her.

Or, perhaps she was crying in exasperation. She could not reconcile herself with the fact that she must spend yet one more Friday night cooking in her own kitchen rather than dining out. Dinner at her favorite restaurant, the Walpack Inn, was no longer allowable, not during this stage of the pandemic.

Maybe she was crying because she had just found out she would not be getting the deposit back on her daughter's lavish wedding, plans which would now be scrapped entirely because the young couple had come to realize, during their time quarantined together, that they don't really like each other well enough to spend the rest of their lives as a married couple.

I felt sorry for the woman. She had lost so much. She had lost, not just the once-in-a-lifetime chance to wear the lavender mother-of-the-bride dress that she had already taken to the tailor's for alterations, she lost the chance to show off the ballroom dancing skills she'd hoped she and her husband would finally master—and she'd just convinced him to start classes next month. The dance studio was closing.

She'd also lost her last opportunity to attend a cherished family event before her own mother succumbed to her advancing dementia.

And she'd lost what was possibly her daughter's last chance for a good match. She was getting so picky, and thirty-six already! The thwarted mother-in-law had looked forward to continuing to brag to her bridge club about her daughter's groom. Her now ex-future-son-in-law had been at the Rutgers School of Medicine and Dentistry and was destined to graduate in less than a year. His mother-in-law-to-be's plans for him were that he was to become an endodontist and take over his father's practice.

And, he was from such a good family!

I think of the Bubonic Plague. The Black Death. There was a time when things were worse. There had been a pandemic which kept returning over the course of centuries, during a time when no one had any idea as to what caused the illness or how to treat it. They could only guess at how to prevent it—and even the best minds of the time guessed wrong, over and over. People died by the millions—from the illness, as well as from its complications, the numbers compounded by a lack of medical knowledge and trained caregivers. And people who were otherwise physically healthy died from violence, as people's ignorance led to incorrect guessing as to the cause of the plague, which led to a breakdown in the social order and the random mass murder of innocents.

I vowed to not cry. The nurse meant well, and she was a hero, working in healthcare in close proximity to people—hazardous at any time. People encountered in a health-care setting tend toward being contagious, some with things that can kill you.

Members of the general public at any time might behave unpredictably. This young woman was risking her health and safety every time she showed up at work, and today she looked cheerful, even though her assigned task meant coming in contact with people and their germs during a deadly pandemic. I did not want to upset her by acting like a big, blubbering baby.

As she neared my car, the white stick was pointing out in front of her. It looked to me like a jousting lance held by an armored knight on his white steed as he approached the Black Knight ... held firmly in the crook of his right arm ... steadied by his gloved right hand ...

I decided to pretend I was a British war bride and follow the advice it is said they were all given on their wedding nights. I shut my eyes, and thought of England ...

Surprisingly, the stab—I mean, the swab—did not hurt.

Lotte Bloom: Her Escape From Nazi Germany

After watching a video of my neighbor's great-aunt,
"Lotte Bloom – Her story of escaping Nazi Germany –
Part 1," YouTube, June 16, 2015
—https://youtube.com/watch?v=f3ap92UIqpk

In a video recording of her interview with a member of her family, Lotte Bloom, originally from Talheim, tells the story of why she left Nazi Germany in 1939 on the final ship to the United States.

Lotte is an eloquent yet natural speaker, describing events from her vantage point as a teenager. She recalls a sudden hostility, which appeared virtually overnight, against herself and her well-respected and much-loved family, from people in the community—friends, neighbors, classmates, and business associates with whom she and her mother and father had been intimate friends. None of them had seen it coming.

Institutionalized hostility toward Jews was compounded by fear that the same horror would happen to anyone—and their loved ones—if they did not participate in this persecution, or at least if they failed to remain silent in its terrible shadow.

Lotte expresses compassion for those who feared that the same would happen to them if they failed to do what they were told. Yet, she shares her deep gratitude for those whose individual actions kept her alive, despite the failure of the larger society.

Lotte became separated from her parents, who were deported to Poland and murdered, but she managed to make it to America. She describes her deep appreciation for those who continued their support for the persecuted.

An oft-repeated line in Lotte's story implies that, though she was targeted for atrocities perpetrated by her fellow human beings, she was somehow sheltered by the divine.

"And, I sometimes wonder, who was looking out for me?"

Love Letter to a Local Minor Poet

When I first heard the words "I've been a poet, now, for twenty-eight years," I could hardly believe the aura of peace in the voice, the reflection in the shining, lively eyes. The speaker shone before me in the beautiful flesh.

I had never before heard the words "I am a poet" from a living soul, nor dared think such an adventure possible. I had believed that those myriad ancient "poetry" books had to have been filled with lies, the wild imaginative flights of the degenerate, the undisciplined, the delirious. Opium eaters, every one.

I'd not been "exposed" to poetry except in the classroom, a mandatory exercise designed to teach the young how to be, how to "know thine enemy"—in our case, the snoot-nosed Brits—and surpass them in refinement.

Most important—heed!—we'd all learned to walk on stilts. The careening toward purest sensitivity precluded any sole-to-earth contact, any passion. Most prized was the wise dry of civility. "Poetry" was a non-entity. The dose of an ode was swallowed under pinched nose from the third row seat, second in, my English teacher poised for the expected yawn. I eagerly slept through any poem said aloud.

I had heard the phrase "Dead Poets" applied to a pretentious pool of names disdained by the walking stilts around me. The movie with the lame name *Dead Poets Society* had to be cliché, flopped out by the pristine-clean Hollywood machine, to be wiped under the armpits of the not-yet-amassed masses it ought to have suited. Such a movie must be made, to fill in gaps, lacks-of-understanding, with fluffed-up popcorn bits. It would easily appease and fool, spawn more falsely-held expectations of "what poetry is." A something called "society" would still be clueless.

Poetry lived and breathed, yes, but hidden in the deepest, darkest dungeons of my soul, held fast in chains of "perfect attendance," "college preparation," "be a good example to your siblings," and sufficient feigned "piety" to cement one's permanent record.

I read no one's "poetry." Such verse must have been penned by the helpless who wished to be thought great, to gain love or respect or sex. The elbows of poets pushed aside the red roses centerpiece, which had been placed, just so, to improve the dinner table. A "poet" always leaned in, with casual conversation, in callous disregard for decoration and decorum.

Who issued licenses to poets to preach to unconscious, sleeping choirs the lie, "Our shit does not stink"? Who were they? Who wrote these "poems"? Those with little regard for human dignity. Out of touch, they stooped to cater to masses.

Actual feelings must remain hidden!

That was all that was deemed proper in the world I inhabited. In the busy world, dreams were things announced at dinner tables; the preceding dollar signs, loosely attached; gilded reflections glistened in the eyes of the attentive; family members steamed in private pride.

Supposedly made for me and mine, *Dead Poets Society* would likely merely trivialize and demean that sensitivity I idolized, conceive excuses, and overdevelop clever lies. Not meant to help us see, the movie would attempt to tug at our heartstrings.

But, mine, I cleverly kept intact and pure. I would not be taken in by *Dead Poets Society*, would not be misled into a false awakening. I refused to see it. Others I admired praised *Dead Poets Society*, but I kept quiet.

Instead, I lived it, inside; my eyes tight closed. I would not see that movie, trash or not. I could not be free, for poetry, until I could climb through that rocky tunnel myself, escape Plato's cave on my own and feel the sun beat my own face.

I had no map, but I followed you, poet-of-twenty-eight-years-and-counting, and today I am unleashed.

This! This is that place, the land above the underground fire, where dancers danced, but only the blind could see.

Here today are all of you, my dead poets, who live and breathe and feel and write—and share. We are gathered; you are dead, like me, to a world we left behind. You, who live tangential to that old lifeless tune, that endless, monotonous drone.

When I first heard the words, "I've been a poet, now, for twenty-eight years," I sat up and listened. Our eyes, the poet's and mine, gleamed, as one.

Like Odysseus, I am, finally, home.

At home, I'm writing poetry. Home and free, I'm allowing myself to be me, a poet.

Mass Incarceration: The Threat Hits Close to Home

My sister once mentioned that jail was her worst nightmare, but I had no idea where that came from. When she was in law school, she'd heard horror stories from many of the incarcerated. But I'd never understood why she, an honest, law-abiding citizen, would fear going to jail.

When she got a speeding ticket in Virginia and a notice to appear in court, like any lawyer, she researched the likely outcomes. In preparation for her court date, she got a five-hundred-dollar haircut and bought new shoes. She drove down to Virginia two days early. She wanted to appear poised and well-rested in front of the judge. She dressed in her best lawyer's suit and the expensive, professional high heels. She applied seven layers of flawless make-up, then showed up in court, prepared for the worst.

Of the twenty-nine traffic cases heard that morning before hers, twenty-nine defendants were escorted out in handcuffs. No exceptions, the law was clear. The penalty for driving twenty miles an hour over the speed limit in a construction zone was thirty days in jail.

My sister pled her case as convincingly as any lawyer, though she hadn't yet passed the bar. She apologized for speeding, calmly, just this side of profusely, and explained how out of character her behavior had been; she was normally a careful driver. She described her trip that day, how she'd left her house in Tennessee when her husband had announced his intention to file for divorce. She'd been heading to her mother's house in New Jersey, crying and upset, though she realized there was never an excuse for speeding, especially in a construction zone—what if it *hadn't* been a Saturday and there *had* been workers present? If anything had happened to anyone due to her negligence, she could not have lived with herself.

She thanked the officer for taking her off the highway before anyone got hurt. She promised she would go back to driving the way she normally does, extremely carefully. She thanked the judge for listening, and said she was ready to accept whatever he decided. She then stood silently, hands folded in front of her.

As the bailiff prepared the handcuffs, the judged asked him to wait a minute. He had a small conference at the bench with the court clerk, then pronounced judgment.

He felt this defendant was repentant, and had been properly chastised by the experience of being arrested and brought to court. He further found she posed no danger to the community.

She put the fine on her credit card and headed home.

She told me she'd bought those heels especially for this hearing. In them, she could have easily rushed the bench without tripping. Her plan was to jump the bailiff, grab his gun, and shoot someone, anyone, inside the courtroom. She'd wanted to be sure she'd be gunned down before she could reach her car in the parking lot.

She was not going to jail.

Music Resets My Headspace

Music, I love, but as far as Leonard Cohen was concerned, no one I knew had ever mentioned him. I'd never heard his name until he was gone. Actually, I'd never paid attention to the names of any bands or musicians or the titles of songs. I just listened to, and loved, all music.

I got my first electric device where I could control the incoming sound myself when my great-aunt died and my parents gave me her clock radio. I was in the fourth grade and heard popular music, rock and roll, for the first time. I lived in a neighborhood where kids played outside and no one could afford to buy records, so mostly, I read books. But I adored my radio.

My parents did own a record player, and "Einekleinenachtmusik" was my mom's favorite album, but I loved them all. Back then, I didn't know music could be identified with a composer like books had a particular author. Of the albums, I could name only Vivaldi's "The Four Seasons" and Holst's "Mars."

My dad liked to play Burl Ives, the Smothers Brothers, and Peter, Paul and Mary. But, more importantly, he played his guitar in the living room, and we'd sing along for hours to his southern spirituals and protests, Pete Seeger, Joan Baez, and folk songs.

I had terrific music teachers in public school. I sang in the madrigal select choir and was first chair first flute in high school. I shared a room with four sisters who insisted on their own music, so I rarely had the luxury of being the one to select the radio station. And it didn't matter. I happily listened to anything, as long as it was music.

I had a limited, but varied, musical education, mostly classical: my own performance on flute and singing in choirs. I still sing with the Sussex County Oratorio Society.

When I was younger, I always listened to O.P. music—Other People's music—in cars or in my crowded house or in the houses of the people I babysat for. My dad grew up during The Great

Depression and was very careful in how he taught us to save, and not spend, money, but whenever I had a nickel, he encouraged me to buy a 45 at the Farmer's Market. All they sold were discards from jukeboxes. I was so proud of my collection of twenty-two terrific hits.

I never had enough money to buy an album until I worked in a department store after high school. I eventually acquired ten albums, bought on sale where I worked. When I had my kids, my two-year-old dropped the needle from my first record player, which I had just bought, down the furnace vent on the floor. I haven't played a record since.

I bought 500 songs on iTunes, not even scratching the surface of what I want to hear. I never play them.

I wake up every day with music in my head. I will never be without music. Music is an opiate. I forget everything else, and it's even dangerous for me to play music on the radio when I drive—I forget where I'm going. My brain is 95% wired to music, and I've got the best music in the world in there.

But, no, I'd never heard the name Leonard Cohen until he died and I read my poetry husband's lament on Facebook, which tore out my guts. My poem "Hallelujah" is included in a Leonard Cohen anthology.

Music resets my headspace, in a good way. Whenever I enter the world of music, the rest of the material world ceases to exist.

My Kingdom, for Paper and a Pen

Note to self: Backing up your computer may not be the perfect solution to saving data, but it is better than not backing up.

My old computer died slowly, from lack of storage capacity. I had no real warning that anything was amiss. It just ran slower and slower, until one day it simply stopped responding.

I originally thought it was a problem with the fan, as the machine started heating up tremendously, to the point where it was so hot I could not use my laptop on my lap. The post-mortem by a professional showed there was no free disk space, and despite all efforts to clean it out and revive it, it never ran well again. In the process of trying to "fix" it myself first—by deleting things—I had made one simple keystroke mistake and lost everything I had ever saved electronically, including about 4,000 original haiku.

I vowed to learn from this horrible experience and never repeat whatever mistakes I had made. First, I switched brands of computer. My next computer had more memory and storage than I imagined I could ever possibly use up, no matter how many photos I took.

Who knew home videos were coming? Who knew I would one day be writing a 200-page book and saving each day's version under a different file name, just in case I wanted to go back and check an older version and revert to an old line or two?

Then, one day, this new-and-improved computer started acting up. Remembering the trouble I had had with the last model, and not recalling the solution—and suddenly remembering there wasn't a successful resolution while still using the same device … it died!—I panicked.

I realized I had to begin saving my documents extra carefully. Immediately.

At the time, I was working on a project under a strict deadline. I was trying to get the first book I had ever written, a poetry book, formatted and sent out for printing. I had less than two days: the printer had promised that my order for hardcover books could be delivered in time to give as gifts for an upcoming family reunion. I had zero time for trouble-shooting.

I could have used an external hard drive or a thumb drive. But, no, I thought to myself, Why not give in and finally make use of modern technology? The cloud has surely been perfected by now! It seemed a reasonable assumption, and the only reasonable alternative. I have misplaced every hard drive and thumb drive I've ever saved precious data on. I could not "misplace" the cloud.

I started emailing myself a copy of whatever I was working on. I have five different email addresses—each one has given me grief in its own unique way. I thought, if the computer dies, at least I have my work saved in two different places, one email In-box and one email Sent-box. You never know when one of the email addresses might fail to fulfill its promise of keeping my messages. I kept switching between the five addresses, just in case.

I did not have an external hard drive backup. Years before, after I had gone back to the store to ask the tech geniuses to investigate the possible causes of the first computer's slowdown and eventual grind to a halt, while I was waiting for my appointment I had swapped horror stories with another customer in line. He had always carefully backed up his data on the company's recommended external device, the one I had been considering. It was supposed to automatically back up everything immediately as it was typed and store it safely until needed. Which it did, just fine, until, one day, this external device glitched and fried. All the saved data on it was suddenly toast. However, the device did not stop working. It continued the backup process until it had completely fried all of the data, not only on this device, but also on everything connected to it: the computer, the cloud, everything. All his data, everywhere: lost, in one fell swoop.

I decided to forego the "automagic" data backup device.

Neither did I have my data automagically backed up in the cloud. The first and last time I had done that, I had hit the wrong button on my computer by mistake, erasing all of my phone contacts, and—surprise, surprise—it immediately compounded my error by erasing all of my phone contacts simultaneously from both my phone and from the cloud. As if I meant to do that. With not even a prompt—"Are you sure you want to erase five years worth of carefully collected data?" Nope. All gone.

Yet, I am out of practice for writing things down to be saved in ballpoint ink. I couldn't find an elephant in the piles of paper I have stored in my house, saved "just in case" I should ever need to go back and find a hard copy of something "important." Writing things down only works for people who are organized within the physical space they inhabit. I am very organized on an electronic device. That is, as long as the device cooperates and does not erase itself.

I somehow once fell under the enchantment of the time-saving mantra "Never touch a piece of paper twice"; now I just jot all vital info directly into my phone. I transfer it to save in an appropriate file on my computer later, at a more convenient time. My life goes into my phone. My phone is normally my lifeline when I need to retrieve something I can't recall at the moment, and now that I can save so much electronically, I remember less and less in my actual physical brain.

When this latest meltdown was occurring and I realized my computer was acting up and not always giving me back the documents I had carefully saved, I came to an awareness that maybe I shouldn't have saved so many versions of the same huge document to a measly machine. It finally dawned on me that this activity might have filled up the storage to overflowing; except, a computer will never understand the concept of "overflowing." When it is out of space, it is out of space. It does not look around to see if there might be an extra empty bucket or two lying around somewhere in the garage that it can use temporarily until it can get to Home Depot and buy some more. But it doesn't tell you it is full. It still says, "Saved successfully" and figures that you will understand later that it tried valiantly to save your valuable data exactly where you told it to, but it had no idea of what Plan B was supposed to be, if it couldn't find room.

I recognized that I was in a computer emergency situation. I might have to stop editing the current project I was working on and send it immediately to the printing company before the computer crashed. It seemed imminent, that disaster was about to take all of my hard work and flush it down the data drain.

I started checking through my phone Contacts, where I had stored extra Notes regarding printing costs, copyright registration, and all the other details I needed to know in order to perform the steps I had to do to get this project finished and out the door. I wanted to see whether there was anything else I needed to research before packaging up the book and waving it goodbye, seeing it off to begin the next leg of its journey from writer to reader.

I realized that, if I wrote any new documents and saved them on the computer, it might run out of room and the computer might die, so I started saving everything only on my phone. I stopped backing up my phone Notes onto the computer, at least until I could get to the point where the data storage crisis was managed.

After about a week of putting everything important into my phone and not into my computer, and checking each of my Notes, my to-do lists of tasks to complete in preparation for the publication of my book, I went back to my phone to read again one of the Notes, a shopping list to which I had added an item just the day before. Not only was the item not on the shopping list, but the shopping list Note on my phone—the one Note I had been using consistently and updating at least once a week for the past two years—had apparently disappeared from the list of Notes on my phone.

Strange.

After only a few minutes investigation, I discovered that every Contact and every Note I had opened during the prior week had vanished—even ones to which I had not made any edits. Some I had just opened to read, and then closed again when I confirmed the data was correct. There were many tasks to be completed: copyright registration, saving the text and cover design to a memory stick, delivering the memory stick to the printer, saving a copy of the text in a format suitable for publication as an e-book. During that week, whenever I had clicked "Create Note" or "Edit Note" or "Contact," and then hit "Save," I had always received the "Saved successfully" message, which had assured me things were working as planned—yet somehow these Notes and Contacts I had "Saved successfully" were gone from the phone.

With. Out. Warning.

After more trouble-shooting, I found that I had totally used up my "free" storage space on the server in the cloud where my phone company stores my data. It was a really large-sized space that I had calculated should have lasted me a lifetime. However, the additional emails I had been sending to myself, of huge documents—my whole book, and many times; and Photoshopped picture files—had been added to that cloud storage area every time I had used the email address associated with my phone. Without warning, after I had reached the storage limit, the devices that were attached to this special area in the cloud simply stopped saving any of my data. I had expected, wrongly, at least a courtesy call or email to let me know I was approaching my limit, and to prompt me to buy additional space. But no, nothing.

Of course, I now realize in retrospect, of course it would not warn me, since I was not a cloud-storage-paying customer. I had, in good faith, been relying on a ready supply of "free" cloud storage space.

I was out of time for exploring other storage options. I realized that if I could manage to extend the storage space allotted to me by my phone's cloud storage service, my cloud/phone problems might be resolved. I remembered that, if I could figure out how to do it, I could probably buy some additional space, which I now knew I needed.

I clicked on my phone's Settings and proceeded to "Storage" and clicked "Buy more storage." It prompted me for my password. While I never write them down on paper—I lose paper—I do save hints to help myself remember my passwords.

Where are the hints? Well-hidden: in my phone's "Contacts." I opened the Contacts and found the hint, and realized right away that I had to write it down, because if I closed the Contact and the problem was not resolved, that Contact was sure to disappear— with all the others that had gone bye-bye during the previous week.

I found a pen and paper and wrote it down. I went back to Settings and found it had timed me out. I opened Settings again and entered the password.

"Wrong password," the phone admonished me.

Oh, no! Did I not even have the right password? Was my data lost forever because I can't remember where I put the right eight characters? I forced myself to stop panicking, and then guessed, correctly, that I had possibly typed it wrong. I tried again, and it worked.

Now, on, to Payment Options.

"Your credit card number we have saved in our files is past its expiration date. Please enter the required information using a different card."

Of course. I ran to the car, got my purse, found my new card.

"Timed out," complained my phone. I went back into Settings to start over. I entered my password.

No response.

I tried again. No luck.

Then I remembered. In order to save me from hackers, if I try to log in three times in succession unsuccessfully, my phone/cloud company puts a block on my account, and won't let me even try to log in using my password, which THIS TIME I KNOW WHAT MY PASSWORD IS, PLEASE BELIEVE ME AND JUST LET ME LOG IN!

I remembered that the last time that happened, I had to ask the tech geniuses at the mall for help, because I had not written down the correct way to type in my responses to the Security Questions: capitals/lower case? The tech had hit a wrong button—and promptly lost all of my data from my phone and the cloud and my computer, simultaneously. This is what had led me to switch computer brands in the first place.

But now, my phone and its data was ... being held hostage to THAT SAME COMPANY. It was, coincidentally, the manufacturer of my latest phone, and the keeper of all its software.

And my data.

I turned off the phone. The computer. And said goodbye to the project deadline, waving to it wistfully as it went wafting by. Holiday gift-giving season is so-ooo overrated anyway, isn't it?

Two days later, I bravely turned on the phone, hoping for a miracle. Maybe, this time, the phone/cloud company had merely put me in an imposed timeout; I was hoping for a semi-permanent stay of its execution of my data requests. I thought I had read somewhere online, at some point in the recent past, that something along those lines had been made a part of modern security procedures, that the draconian "No, you can't have your own data!" skirmishes of the last data war might be history. I went to Settings, entered my password, and ... it worked! I entered my credit card info to "Buy more storage." Pressed Enter. And ...

Nothing happened. When I backed out through the menus, it still said that I was contracted for the old amount of storage, the "free" storage limit; and that I was still merely 588k shy of reaching that limit.

I refreshed the page by rebooting the phone. Nothing changed.

Recalling that the previous tech geniuses had "solved" my problem by simply creating a new account, I realized that the new account ID and the old account ID might be different for the phone and for the computer, and I knew they had never been successfully linked because, though a "genius" had promised me that I would be able to do that "At any time. We'll come back to that, don't worry!" the company had later said, "Oops, my bad. That's never gonna happen."

Now, I went on the company's website on the computer. I logged in using the phone's ID, but it also did not show a change in the storage capacity. I again went through the process to "Buy more storage" and again entered my credit card info. It appeared to work correctly, yet it still showed I had the same inadequate storage capacity total as it did previously. I logged out, then logged in again, this time using the old account's ID. I went through the process of "Buy more storage" and again it appeared to work—and still, when I checked on the amount of storage in the account, there was no change to the amount of total storage available. I tried again, and this time, the credit card information wouldn't go in.

I shut off the computer and tried the phone. No change.

I shut off the phone.

The next day, I turned on the phone, gingerly. I went to Settings, checked the cloud storage capacity, and ... IT HAD GIVEN ME WHAT I HAD WANTED! Hallelujah! I checked also on the computer, using the other ID, and that page also said that the same, larger, amount of storage was now available. I tested it several different ways, and it also appeared that the phone had started working normally again. As far as I can tell, the phone has not lost any data since then.

Ah, computers! Little, mindless machines. They don't really think for themselves, they only do what we tell them to do. Except that, even if they belong to you, you are only one in a long line of people who has told them what to do. Company engineers write lines and lines of code, then other company engineers rewrite it in an endless stream of "Updates" to bring you new functionality and to fix the innumerable bugs that had previously made it into the code—and none of those other people are telling you exactly what it is that they have instructed your computer to do.

Now I went back onto the computer, to solve its storage problem. I emptied the "Recycle Bin." This seemed to solve the problem right away. At least for the moment, my documents were now saving correctly.

But, when the computer had been sick due to this storage problem, the only clue I had had was that the document I was working on had suddenly lost all of its formatting. And then, when I had closed it, it was no longer there when I tried to open it again.

No problem, I had thought, the document died because the computer ran out of storage. Now that there is plenty of storage, I will simply open up the backup version of the document.

I couldn't find it. The "automatically" backed up document, too, had vanished. It turns out, the file-naming system had run out of space and crashed. The data might be in there, somewhere, but the lights were out as if nobody was home. There was no list anywhere of the "Details" that could have shown me the names of documents hidden in my computer.

The "Search" function on my word processor worked, so I could search for a file by name and it would open, but I had to type in the exact name I had saved it under, which I could not remember. I had decided to use a computer in the first place, rather than writing my book into a series of notebooks I might lose, because I can't remember titles of things I've written and I'm not organized enough to remember where I put them. I thought that's what computers were for. The titles I had randomly given to copies of my book, as I saved them, had names such as "book-v4-copy-GOOD-ready-to-print-REVISED-October 22-b."

Fortunately, I was able to go back into my emails and find copies of my work from the previous weeks leading up to the data disaster. I am still not sure I have the latest version. I am working on reading the version I use now, very carefully, to see if any of the hundreds of recent edits I had made might not be there—but who can remember? My brain is full, and I can't wait to start relying on computers again, though I will never, ever trust one.

I know the truth now, that every time I touch the keyboard— when I make a single keystroke!—I am also kissing my data goodbye. If I really need to know something later, I will take the time and make the effort to actually memorize it.

But, really, life is too short for that.

I do feel sorry for the young, those who are now growing up using computers as their brain's "better half." They may be facing constant disappointment when those digital demons fail to remain faithful to their task of saving, and then giving back, what we have tasked them to remember so that we don't have to. Easy as it is to save data, data retrieval is not to be taken for granted. The Contacts on my phone have, as late, been properly backed up on the phone company's website—but they do not save the Notes I have written in the non-categorized "extra" space, the many lines I have added which contain random information that I want associated with the person who I will need to contact via their phone number. I write those interesting tidbits in the Notes: the extension number of a person's office phone, the birthdays of their three children, the name of the dog hotel they used that was open on Christmas—important details of life that would be nice to remember, but probably you could live without if you forgot. Those Notes are only saved on my phone—which could die— and on the phone/cloud company's server. They are only accessible when using the cloud on the phone or computer or when restoring the Contacts to another phone—but only to a phone which was manufactured by the same company. Apparently, each phone manufacturer has its own method of storing what their phone users ask them to save; each has its own unique software, and none of them talk to the others.

Another victim of the practice email-myself-a-copy-of-whatever-I-am-working-on-so-I-don't-lose-it was my calendar, which I keep on a website I created using a free template and a free hosting service. The data is apparently saved using a cloud storage account, one they've set up to share with my email data and the other data I save on my other personal "free" websites. When I had signed up for this website service, it had been advertised as "unlimited free storage." Sometime during one of the many and frequent "upgrades," and probably hidden deep within the "modified user service agreement contract," must have been a notice that they were going to start limiting the amount of allowed storage, and that it would apply across all products the company serviced.

I think I remember reading something about that, somewhere on the internet, at some time, but I cannot recall any of the specifics. I figured I could always look up the details if I needed to.

Nothing free is ever free, and I would have offered to pay real money for adequate storage, but I still have no idea how to get in touch with this company. It will easily help you to set up a paid business account which comes with customer service, but it leaves voiceless those individuals who might want to pay extra to receive good service, but can't because they are not a "business." I have not been able to find a "Contact Us" page with options for buying adequate customer service, for myself, as an individual. There is no phone number to call. No email address. No "chat" available. Nothing for us "little people."

I have been using this calendar on my computer and on my phone for years, and when it ran out of storage capacity, THERE WAS NO WARNING. As I entered data and hit "Save," the site's messages still cheerfully said "Saved successfully." But, when I went back to read what I had written a week later, nothing had been updated. My recently-entered data was nowhere to be found.

What did I expect? After all, it is just a computer. It only does what hundreds of people, maybe thousands of people, have lined up to tell it to do; me, last in line, of all.

As for my 4,000 "lost" haiku, I had saved them on my computer and lost them in a computer crash. However, I had originally written them, one at a time over the years, on a social media website, and suddenly AND WITH NO WARNING the site had stopped allowing readers to go back and browse old posts that had been written more than a month before. The haiku were probably saved on a server somewhere, but they were inaccessible to me, the author.

It had never occurred to me I could be cut off from reading back my own words, as the site reworked its programming to "improve" the user interface.

However, by happenstance, a few years later, when I had been casually searching the internet to see if I could find my own name, I found about a thousand of these haiku. The poems were saved on a web page entitled "Haiku" and listed me as author - I checked and they were indeed all mine. Luckily for me, I had tagged them #haiku at the time I had posted them, which is what I think may have been their life preserver in the ocean of data from which they were fished. I have no idea who fished them out and saved them or why, but I was so happy to read these old friends, which I thought had been lost forever, it gave me hope that all my other words were also sooner or later going to pop up for me to revisit, and we would soon be happily chatting about old times.

However, the other lovely words I had written and posted on that site remain missing. I had not tagged them. I am sure they are saved somewhere, on a computer data island no longer floating in a data sea, relics rusting on the ocean floor on a beautiful sunken ancient continent called Computer-Never-Never-Again-Will-You-Ever-See-Them Land.

I copied the haiku back from the web page onto my computer. So as not to lose them again, I decided to try to collect them into a book and publish them, on paper, and make them available on Amazon's publish-on-demand site. I wanted to be able to have in hand my poems in a hard copy book. But, in case I ever lost the book, at least I could find the words available, somewhere within the online world, to those willing to pay to access them.

That would be me. Just charge me, I'll pay, I'll pay! Just, please, give me my words back.

Of course, in the process of completing the steps to put my book out there for publication, I crashed my current computer—and my phone, to boot. I think it was for lack of adequate storage. Every digital device I had been relying on for my daily existence was fried. But not before I had saved my work-in-progress off-site, on a new device, one that fit in the palm of my hand.

I carried the thumb drive with the two PDFs,—the carefully-edited text and the book cover I had designed in Photoshop—to a local bricks-and-mortar printer, who successfully delivered me my order. In less than two months, I had, in my hot little hand, 200 gorgeous copies of my first book. I gave them all out to friends and relatives, people I knew I could rely to lend me their copy, once I lost my own.

I have learned a thing or two about digital data back-up: I really have to start writing things down.

On paper.

My Poetry Journey Began With a Stumble

My sixth-grade English teacher accepted my poorly-written first attempt at poetry—even as a classmate, a neighbor of mine and a dear friend, whom I highly respected, shocked me, by mocking me aloud—and, in front of the whole class!—for shirking my duty to properly do my homework in a timely fashion. She had seen me write down the terse twelve lines in a panic, and I had just put down my pen as the teacher came up the aisle. I had handed the teacher my sheet of paper at, literally, the last second.

Ten minutes before, as I had walked into the classroom, I realized I had forgotten to do the assignment. So, I had started scribbling furiously, to bring the poem in under deadline—class was about to start—and my friend saw me.

The girl herself had slaved for hours over her own lovely sonnet. Whereas she prided herself on being responsible, I was always a last-minute student. Yet, my work was consistently rewarded with grades of "A" and she struggled for the teacher's approval.

The girl seemed determined that I would not receive yet another unearned "A" for last-minute work when, obviously, to her, I deserved an "F" for effort.

The girl started in with her complaint immediately when, in turn after she had read hers, I had finished reading my "poem" aloud.

It's obvious!—she demanded, and the teacher must observe—that that horrible excuse for a poem had been written in a rush. It had no consideration for rhyme or meter. She went on to berate me for the poem's cheap brevity, a mere four syllables per line: a construction of time-saving convenience, given the constraints of our assignment demanded a minimum line count of twelve.

She accused me of cheap sensationalism, writing about a dead dog merely to gain the sympathies of the reader—the teacher—who might be convinced to award an "A," if only out of compassion for one who had lost a pet.

"She's never even had a dog!" she informed my peers, who knew she and I were friends who knew each other's secrets. "She doesn't even like dogs!"

I loved cats. My family had always loved cats. I'd never known anyone with dogs. And she didn't have a dog, either. She'd shared that heartbreak with me.

It didn't matter. In front of the whole class, I was revealed for the dog-indifferent poem-less fraud I was.

I don't recall exactly my poem's wording, but this is close:

> *My best friend's dog*
> *had big, red sores.*
> *Her dad drove to*
> *the hospital.*
> *The vet told him*
> *there was nothing*
> *that could be done.*
> *He put Sam down.*
> *My best friend's dad*
> *came home alone.*
> *My best friend and*
> *I cried all day.*

This had been a true story, one this same dear friend had told to me earlier in the week. It had really happened, though not to her, it had happened to her cousin.

It must have broken her heart to hear her own story told in a poem; her words twisted, hiding the origin of the pain. We had both cried, sobbed, screamed, cursed, the day she'd told me of her cousin's loss.

My poem had reached its mark. It had touched my friend, right where it counts. That's what a poem does.

And, as I had been writing the poem in haste, I was not remembering the source of the story, that it was my friend's cousin's dog, or even that the story had come to me from my friend's telling. I recalled only the terrible feeling of being tossed by threatening, high waves while holding onto an unsteady raft, riding out a storm on an ocean of roiling emotion, which had been unleashed by the sudden unexpected loss of a dear loved one. It is that emotion that I had decided to channel, somehow sensing that, somewhere, in there, was a poem.

I had allowed it to be drawn from my pencil onto my blank page, hoping that I could make twelve lines of four syllables happen before the final bell rang and the teacher arrived to collect my homework. I had no lofty goals of being thought a "poet."

The girl was right. When I had started writing, I was indeed in a panic that class was starting and I was unprepared. I needed to write a poem, fast, and I had never written a poem before. I wracked my brain, trying to remember what I had been taught.

What was a poem, anyway?

I knew poems relied on emotions, so I looked inside for something handy, and I had grabbed onto the first raw emotion I saw. I remembered something recently had been very sad, something about someone's dog being sick.

And that explains to me, now, her strong reaction to my words, why they provoked in her such a vehement declamation against their worth.

When I started to write the poem, I was out of time for planning, so I made it up, line by line, as I went along. I kept writing, for twelve lines, carefully using four syllables in each. When I got to the magic twelve, I stopped—and immediately handed in my "work," as the teacher was just at that moment walking past my desk, her hand out to collect my poem.

After my friend's near-hysterical outbreak over my homework fail, the teacher turned her attention to my poem. First, she read it to herself. She paused a moment, then she calmly read my poem aloud. She had recognized the opportunity as a teachable moment, if only because the students were paying attention, due to the drama of my friend's complaint.

The teacher started in and discussed each of the lines of my poem as an illustrative example of the constructs of poetry. How wonderful, how each of the elements in this brief poem illustrated one or another of the great poetic ideals! She remarked on the poem's concise language, which yet contained a full exploration of an extraordinary depth of feeling. She lauded the poet's use of highly descriptive language; and the poet's thematic choice, to use the death of a beloved pet as the subject for a poem. This sort of personal experience is best handled by poetry, above all other forms of literature—such deep emotion demanded focus, requiring brevity of expression. And often, it is too painful to write literally about what truly hurts—poets use metaphor to establish a common understanding with the reader. Here, a poem about man's best friend recognizes the dog as a symbol for love and friendship.

And, certainly, it would have been so much easier for the student to have gone the common route and written a poem which conformed to a standard and familiar form—like a sonnet. It must have taken the writer great courage to explore poetic expression in free verse, to go beyond convention and strike out in originality, into new and uncharted territory. To have written a poem in free verse—she hadn't even taught us yet about free verse. What creativity!

Such an excellent poem!

My friend put her head down and sobbed into her desk.

I was mortified, and swore I would never write another poem, a promise nearly kept.

Never Nervous No More

The reason I am not nervous when I am reading a poem aloud is because I am not up there in front of an audience representing myself, I am immersed in the experience of the poem.

From inside the experience of a poem, one does not see oneself, nor one's surroundings. One does not feel embarrassment. One feels only the expression of the poem, releasing itself into sound, so it can rush into the arms of the listener, who will love it and comfort it and understand it, as it needs to be understood. As the reader, I am detached from the experience—an observer, as the poem reveals its innermost thoughts aloud.

Normally, a poem is not equipped with a voice, it is a bunch of words on paper. When I am reading a poem, I become the voice for the voiceless poem. I am not myself, but I become the poem itself, alive and speaking, and I am telling the audience what I would tell them if we were having a private, intimate conversation where I, the poem, am trying to get my point across, to let the listener know just exactly how I feel and why I feel compelled to speak.

I am an actress, the poem is the character I am playing. But unlike a character, a mere part in a play invented by an author, the poem is real, as a person is real. The poem has something to say, but it is powerless to tell anyone else what it wants to say—unless it finds someone, like me or you, willing to help it, to give it its voice, to let its sound become real. The poem wants to be heard, understood, appreciated. It wants to be made real. Love makes things real.

This is also how I feel as I am constructing a poem. The poem is there. It is real. It has something to say. I am guessing what those words are, right up until I hear the poem say, "Thank you for listening, for getting it right. That is EXACTLY what I meant to say!"

I think this is also true when it comes to acting. No matter what the lines in the play are, I am not myself speaking the lines—so there is no way to judge my performance, and, not being judged, there is no way to become embarrassed. I am the character, the words I say are the character's words, as described by the playwright, and my voice is mouthing the thoughts being channeled to me from that character, from where they stand in their position in the play.

Mindset is a very powerful thing!

New Tricks

Having just been to visit a friend recovering from a stroke in a rehab center, where I had brought her husband to visit her—he had earlier had a stroke and could no longer drive —I realized, I really need my husband to die before me.

Amidst the clinical scent of disinfectant—her house had a hospital recovery room atmospheric squirm—my friend was relearning how to use the toilet and still needed assistance.

I admired the loving way she asked her husband, cheerfully, "Hon, wipe my butt?" as she was still unable to do it herself. How quickly that turned into, "Just do what I tell you!" when he was slow, awkward, ineffectual, or missed his mark. Though he really did try, his right hand had never worked quite the same, not since he'd had that stroke of his own.

He jumped into willingness, in his eagerness to not be abused. "I'll do whatever it takes, my dear, to take care of you, to keep you clean and comfortable!" He could no longer rely on his better half to jump in and help, as she always did. Readily and eagerly, she always did.

Their words hit me in the center of my reality, pitched me into imagining a future where self-determination would be a distant, fond memory. I went home with a newly fully-rounded sense of hopelessness.

It's not just that I'm envious of them, that they can communicate. It's just that my husband and I will *never* share that sort of intimacy, that deepness of trust.

I cannot imagine him *ever* being able to comprehend that such a burden, of caring for someone so intimately—especially if that someone were me—would ever, in any version of reality, have anything to do with *him*, let alone be solely his responsibility.

No One Knows Where I Am

After the first two times he had had to make the two-hour and twenty-minute round-trip journey back home to retrieve his electronic name tag before being granted admittance to his office building, his paranoia about keeping it on him at all times had made him reluctant to part with the device, even to shower, lest he forget to reattach it to his clothing before leaving for work. Now, every morning, his wife clipped his ID tag onto the lapel of Roger's jacket for him before she allowed her husband to kiss her goodbye. It was part of their daily routine.

He joked with her that it was an exercise in futility for the company to think it could control its employees. A fellow worker had confided to him in the lunch room on his first day that, once he had logged into his computer to begin work, he could at any time leave his tag in his desk drawer and wander all around the building. As long as he never attempted to open a door or use the elevator, he could stand near the secretaries to eavesdrop or explore any room left open, and no one would ever know he was AWOL. It was impossible to keep tabs on people by forcing them to wear a name tag monitored by a stupid computer.

Roger bragged to his wife, "I walk around all the time. No one knows where I am."

Even the bathroom doors required authorized access. Couldn't allow just anyone in to poop, Roger acknowledged. Bad for business, you know!

Roger in marketing had been disciplined just last week for having been discovered in an unauthorized area of the corporate complex without the identifying tag on his person. When he showed up at the door to Conference Room 520 in the D-wing at 8:51 a.m., holding his briefcase with his presentation materials and looking quite professional in his new suit, he was quickly escorted by security straight to the visitor's desk at the main entrance to the building.

He missed his meeting.

After a brief discussion, during which much was typed into a computer, an officer walked him back to his office and carefully monitored his search for his electronic tag as a mic relayed his words explaining himself to the supervisor in charge of this building's security. Roger retraced his steps, trying to figure out where and how he had misplaced his name tag; he spoke aloud. As per his employee agreement, his words were recorded. With his permission, which he granted, they might use his words "later for training purposes."

Roger insisted his ID had been in his jacket pocket when he'd arrived at work. His wife was very good about that, making sure he never left home without the card. He admitted he had a terrible memory, but his wife clipped his electronic device onto the lapel of his jacket every morning as she kissed him and got him out the door on time for work. In the three months since he'd started his new job, he'd never been late once. Excepting, of course, those two times when he had had to return home to fetch his electronic ID. That doesn't happen anymore, Roger insisted.

Today, as usual, he'd come through the revolving door into the main lobby without incident. He'd entered the elevator, arrived on the fourth floor, said hello to the receptionist, and chatted a minute or two with Carol from finance. Her cold was better—she had all but stopped sneezing.

Roger had opened his office door and dropped his briefcase on his desk. All, as usual. At no time had anything beeped nor any guard ask him to drop what he was doing and allow himself to be led to the security clearance area.

He must have had his ID on him. It was the only way the building's security system could have verified his identity and run his agenda through the corporate database and assured his presence was expected at each stop along the way. When he arrived at a checkpoint, an electronic monitor confirmed he was to be allowed entrance, then the automatic door would open. All sections of the complex but the lobby off the visitor's parking lot were clearly marked as areas where admittance was reserved to "Authorized Personnel Only."

He'd hung up his jacket on its proper hook on the coat rack in the corner by his third-floor office window. When he left his office to go to his meeting, he had put the jacket on and fastened the middle button.

Roger could not fathom how it was possible that his ID tag was not securely clutching his lapel. He checked his pockets, and rechecked. Every pocket was empty.

The security officer was not new to his job. He asked whether Roger had brought his lunch in a bag. Whether he had carried in with him that morning a bag with gym clothes. There must have been something else he had been carrying, something that still held his ID-tag. Had he handed off anything to another employee?

The two of them looked around the spare room. Roger had only recently finished orientation and the training program for his new position and been given his own office. There were no extra bags in sight, no piles of books, no hats or gloves, no umbrellas, no boots. On the desk was a phone and a photo of his wife. His car keys were in his pants pocket.

Ah, but there, hanging on a hook on the coat rack was a raincoat. One Roger did not recognize.

Roger had no idea how it had gotten there, but when the guard checked the lapel, there, on its metal ring, was clipped the plastic-coated tag, "Roger Clemens."

Roger was very good at his job, but he knew he had a terrible memory. However, of one thing he was certain: he had never worn a raincoat. He didn't own one.

He tried to piece together the events of the morning. The raincoat was wet; it had been raining. As he had walked out the door of his house to leave for work, he had kissed his wife. He remembered his wife rushing him to his car—he was almost running late. She had delayed him a few extra minutes before they got out of bed. He blushed as he remembered; his wife had given him an extra surprise for his birthday.

His birthday! So eager was Roger to make his first big presentation at work that morning, he had all but forgotten.

It was his birthday. His wife had kissed him and said, "Happy Birthday!" again when he'd left for work.

When he had left for work, it had been raining. The windshield wipers had been flapping, reminding him he had been meaning to take the car in for service and get them replaced. He was probably also overdue for an oil change. They would check their computer and let him know.

But, his jacket was dry, while the raincoat was wet.

Though he had never owned a raincoat, he must have worn this one. Puzzled, he stared at it. He did not remember shopping for a raincoat. He was sure he'd never seen this one before.

Of course! His wife had given him the new raincoat for his birthday that morning, just as she was rushing him out the door. She hadn't yet had a chance to wrap it, but when she saw it was raining, she decided she didn't want to wait until after dinner. She hadn't yet made the cake.

A man should be dry when he goes to work to support his wife, and, especially, a special man, on his special day.

She'd put his arms through the sleeves of the coat, buttoned it up as she kissed him—extra for his birthday—and pushed him out the door with a smile and a promise more was to come. At work, he'd taken it off and hung it up before taking off the jacket.

He'd never actually looked at this birthday present, though he'd gotten excited thinking about what more would be coming later after he blew out the candles after dinner.

For the rest of the morning, he'd been so focused on his upcoming presentation, intent on rehearsing what it was he was going to say in the opening words, that he'd practically floated through on auto-pilot.

The early morning thunderstorm had been unexpected, and when he arrived at his assigned parking spot with only a minute to spare, he'd grabbed his briefcase and hurried, trying to dance around the puddles. He did not have a spare dry pair of shoes to change into. A late arrival would have warranted an extra stop at the front desk to explain himself and to verify his identity to the satisfaction of the uniformed staff. It was their job to assure that only those who belonged were granted admittance to the building and those inside were all in their allotted slots, at all times verified to be where they were supposed to be.

Security. No matter what else one did for J Corp, keeping the company secrets was the one part of the job description that was non-negotiable. People with electronic IDs traveled freely from car to elevator to swivel chair, but the data they worked with was secured in silicone handcuffs and its path carefully monitored.

The real challenge to the corporation was to contain the intelligence so carefully won, to preserve the integrity of the company's assets. Wireless devices recorded every movement throughout the money-making Wonderland in real time, but, even so, it was difficult enough to account for human stupidity, error, and sloth. Running down the whereabouts of a rogue electronic tracking device was its own special hell.

To make sure no one shared one iota of J Corp's collective knowledge with any entity in the outside world, for either fun or profit, J Corp had hired Ilsa, Inc, a firm which manufactured electronic handcuffs, sold the integrated computer systems which assured their proper use, and held regular trainings to assure continued employee compliance.

Roberta from Human Resources made the arrangements. Roger was signed up for an obviously necessary refresher with Ilsa.

Not One of the Usual Suspects

I quickly chewed and swallowed a stick of gum, flushed the evidence, and stayed in the stall during the berating.

After the others were sent back to class and all was quiet, I came out. The teacher was still there, hands akimbo—until she saw it was me. Then, she relaxed her stance.

I never missed a beat. Before she could utter a word, I breathed a loud, obvious sigh of relief, smiled at her broadly, and blurted out my rehearsed spiel.

"Oh, I'm so glad they left! I hate the smell of smoke. The bathroom gets so smoky, smoke gets in my clothes. I don't want to smell like a smoker!"

The teacher assured me—no one would think I was a smoker.

If I die of Coronavirus, people would not suspect me of breaking quarantine.

"Not her!" they'd say, "She's always been one of the good kids."

On Looking Tasty

A s I walked through the red door at the front of the frat house at the invitation of a high-school acquaintance—a squeaky-clean guy with a pleasant face and a clean reputation—I was eyed up and down by a beer-infused mob. It was noted quite clearly (over the loudspeaker) that I did not have an escort, and my classmate admonished his brothers, "You have to watch out for her. She's a good kid. I'm not kidding!" Each "brother" greeted me warmly, friendly and casual. None looked like the dateable kind who would strike up a conversation to see where it went, but I could not have foretold I would be passed out cold after one beer and wake the next day with my clothes on inside out. I continue to hate the word "brother" even today, and I never let my kids join teams or clubs or any other clan that manifests collective pride in anything resembling that fulsome, fraternizing sort of group think that would encourage objectifying a person; and I do hope that high-school kid's sweet, impish grin really was one born of innocence.

Walking Newark's streets on machinery row with ten minutes to go before I got to the office, I was eyed up and down by a poorly-shod street rat and told, "Honey, you look like breakfast in bed!" I never let show on my face my heat, nor did I slip in my stride, but my heart skipped a beat at the impertinence. I knew I could outrun him, if it came to it, but that one event made me change my plans.

I spiced up my résumé, and made for life in the burbs.

Walking in the country, on my street, down to the dead end, I was eyed up and down by a wild cat; not a stray become feral, but a very large feline with tall, pointed, tufted ears, of a breed that seemed to belong with the worst of the beasts, one who could hang with the meanest in the trees, one who would drag littler, weaker creatures with freshly-snapped necks up to higher branches, to save for snacks later.

I may have looked like lunch on the fly, but I stared down the bobcat, who let us pass, my little dog and I. I grinned with relief at our narrow escape.

I picked up the pace and put extra space between me and my predacious new friend. But I recalled all the times I'd been harassed, seen as fresh meat, and left panting from fright, with my tongue hanging out.

I grew thirsty—for revenge!

On Mute, There's Still That Look on Your Face

My dog bounds in from the kitchen, nails "Clip-pitty! Clip-pitty!" on the dining room hardwood floor.

I'm on mute and the poets on Zoom don't hear his frantic scratching on the front door, his throwing up on the living room rug—before I can even stand up—or my husband cursing as he rushes in from the bedroom.

The neighbor kids suddenly shriek, in tandem, "Quit it!" "Quit it? No, you quit it!"

A random "Ow!"

A scream. "Mommmm! He's doing it again!"

"What is it, Sweetie?"

"I had it first!" "So?" "So, it's my turn!"

"Let your sister have a turn on the sled."

Scree-ee-eech! Ooo-oof!

"Ow! Stop!"

"Mom!" "Mom!"

"Now-www . . . Be nice!"

One and One-Half Digits Short

I asked you why you had only one pinkie and why you were missing one half of the middle finger on your other hand.

You told me you once knew someone who had explained to you in clear language—poetically clear language—what it was they wanted you to do, but you failed to understand what it was they intended. Their exact words: "It's cold out there!"

When writing poetry, we use every one of the exact words we need, but not one extra. Poets cut the extraneous. If a poem were a piece of meat, we'd keep everything that's good to eat and discard the rest.

At my poetry workshop, we slash lines from each other's poems. We remind each other to "cut right up to the bone."

Poets are careful when we write. If we make a poor word choice—or, we out leave a word or two—something vital is lost.

Pet Vacations

When pets go on vacation—and, face it, who doesn't need a break from those who own us?—they set off in packs so they won't get lost. They don't all know the way to get home. They buddy up and count noses and fins and tails and beaks and talons and scales. The Animal Kingdom takes a census, now and then, and animals know who is who, even if humans can't always tell.

They wait for the moon to rise—they're afraid of the dark—and it's got to be a full moon on a cloudless night. The cicadas provide cover, screeching as the rest flee, so humans won't discover the plot from a squeak in the floorboards, a tiny footstep or slither, or a flutter out of the ordinary.

Their wild friends help them escape from their cages, open the tricky locks that block their way. There's no place so secured, that, at least once before, a spider hasn't already been able to get inside; nothing so intact, that bacteria haven't been able to breach the perimeter and ooze their way in. And, those who are skilled, through practice, at getting into confined spaces, can easily help a friend in a pinch figure out a way to get themselves out. Those creatures who always have plenty of free time are happy to stick around all night, and they lead the tamed back in, before dawn.

So, if you are awake after twilight and the moon is full and there's not a cloud in sight and the cicadas are screeching, and, other than that, you don't recognize any noise, like your pet snoring, and you know you're too boring for your pet to bear 24/7/365, year after year—stay in bed. Don't get up to sneak a peek through the blinds for a glimpse at the shed under that tree with the vines. You might see a shadow, or three, creeping through the shrubbery and believe you have an intimate familiarity with a paw or the twitch of an ear on one of the critters—

Wait, who is that? Are they running a six-legged race in the grass?

It's your pets, going out to their secret place where they dance the macarena. But they'll be done having fun, back at home before the sun calls you out of bed to fill their bowls, as usual, with their favorite breakfast grub. And, come morning, you'll notice an extra crinkle—from a broader smile—in the corner of one of your pet's eyes.

If it has eyes. And, if you're very observant.

Your pet will seem happier and more relaxed. But don't even try to find out why. Even if you ask, a pet will remain mum. They won't explain a thing.

What happens in the shed, stays in the shed.

Pictures at a High School Band Concert

My piccolo shrieked "Stars and Stripes Forever" as if I had written it. The music marched through the county park.

We moved past Sousa to Mussorgsky. I turned page after page marked "Flute 1," piece after piece, sweating in the sun in my folding chair, wearing the floor-length white gown I made in Home Ec.

As the girl in First Chair began her classical solo, her head bobbed and her flute swayed gracefully in time to the waltz. I relaxed and laid my flute in my lap.

The afternoon crowd in the park and I soon sat enraptured. I imagined Victorian ladies and gallant gentlemen pointing their toes and curtsying, dancing the minuet in elegant lines, the ballroom curtained in purple velvet.

A big, hairy moth landed on my glasses. Horrified, I batted it away.

It came back, and entangled itself in my long, blonde hair. Not wanting to touch it with my fingers, I swung my head violently to shake it out. I grabbed a piece of sheet music and swept it away. It disappeared behind the music stand.

Just in time, before the end of the solo and the orchestra's entrance, I found my place in the music.

I raised my flute to my lips.

The moth reappeared, fluttering on the end of the soloist's flute. Intensely focused on her performance, she never saw it. But, when she inhaled deeply for the trilled run, the moth disappeared. And she began sputtering!

Pig Roast in an Abandoned Farmer's Field, 1979

It was a party thrown by a gang in an abandoned farmer's field. A real gas. A roasted pig, whole, spitted, fitted over a charcoal pit filled with twigs, leaves, and logs, and lit.

They circled the pig, the biker gang. Drunk and high, and with bloodshot eyes. Enthralled by flames. Choking on smoke.

Entranced by the light, they danced to the beat of the sizzling fat. Oozing squeals of delight, they watched the pig fry. Hissing, sizzling, spritzing fat. Pig smell, roasting, rose through the night.

They added their own music: screams, pain, pure fright. Taking turns, they beat each other bloody raw, whichever of their buddies were within reach. They got out their toys. Leather belts. Metal buckles. Brass knuckles. Their teeth.

The exhibition fights added game to the summer night.

Then, the fire stalled. By midnight, misty fog and light rain had tamed the flames. A bald, raunchy guy in a black leather vest tended the fire. He screamed at a scrawny kid to fetch more gas from the barn. The boy brought cans full of gas. The gas was for the Harley hogs. The man fed it to the flames instead.

He upturned a box and squeezed, squirting gas onto the pyre. It brought the fire back to life. He doused the smoldering, damp twigs and the log. He poured a steady line of gas, back and forth along the spine from snout to tail, then drenched the top of the pig's head. The flames reignited the hair on the ears.

The container swept back and forth. More and more gasoline. Flames leapt higher and higher. The tail of the hog ignited. Flames shot straight up in the air.

A cheer rose from the hungry men gathered around. They were anxious for the cook to tell them it was time to dig in. They wanted meat. Switchblades sprung open.

Impatience hovered like murder hornets. The cook sliced off an ear. It wasn't done. He poured on more gas.

A flash enveloped the burning snout. After the flash, a streak. The skin on the pig's spine split open. Fat burst into flame. Higher and wider and longer, flames filled the hog's bed. From head to tail along the spit, it was one long glow in the night. The streamed gasoline, soaking the skull of the beast, blazed as a ball.

Still, the cook poured, streamed and streamed the gas, more and more.

Then, an arrow of flame shot up from the pit to the can in his hand. The cold of the night split wide open.

Blast!

The can exploded so fast, it ignited the sky. Burst into a fireworks display. The man's screaming lingered, shrieks echoed, as he ran through the field, streaming flames, round in circles ... screaming ... screaming ... screaming.

Screaming ... screaming ... screaming ...

Until, behind a hill, he disappeared from sight. Mass peals of laughter followed, spilt from bikers' split sides. Shrieks pierced the night. Those bikers bellowed in delight. Giddy tears of glee, gleaming, streamed down their cheeks.

The traces of water reflected pure red from flames still blazing in the field ... now crossing the grass ... now racing toward the horizon ...

Flames of burning coils of hay circled the sky. The night sky blazed with light, as if day.

Poster Child

I feel like a poster child for the #MeToo movement, though my story is so much less compelling than that of so many others.

One man came up to me after I delivered my poem describing sixteen of the sexual assaults I experienced, which were of varying degrees of severity, to tell me, "You'd never know, from looking at you."

No wonder women are silent. People expect to see the face of a victim, not a competent, confident, successful—or a normal and ordinary—woman, man, or child.

It is hard to describe to others, without tears, what has happened. The anger, the fear, and the horror are ever-present at these memories. We do not forget. It is nearly impossible to speak of a single rape—much less, a string of, a lifetime of, assaults—without tears, without breaking down in a vulnerable hush, a heap of limping, whimpering, soul-crushed mush.

It is harder to hear that women brave enough to come out as "raped" are not believed; that rapists are not apprehended and taken off the streets and taught how not to rape again. That people still think an assault victim wears a cowl of shame—she bows her head, averts her eyes to avoid public scrutiny of her pain. That she cannot possibly heal. That she will always find it difficult to mingle with strangers and nearly impossible to interact with others with trust.

It must show on her face. It must!

But, no, that is not the case. There might be visible indications that one has been been sexually abused, and some did appear, in my case. But these signs have mostly dissipated over time.

It is hard to walk around in public, knowing that a woman or man you might meet has been raped, or has experienced any physical, mental, or sexual abuse—but might not have even told anyone—and that you can't see it in their face. It is hard to know there are people, whether they have been publically identified or not, who have sexually abused or assaulted someone—who do not have anyone with whom they can talk to about it, no one to whom they can admit their transgression and ask for help in their efforts to reform. They cannot even attempt to atone or make amends, not even to say, "I'm sorry," without fear of legal repercussions.

They have hurt someone. Why do we assume they are incorrigible, intransigent, determined to exercise their right to violate again? How many do seek a way to stop—to gain a deeper understanding of why they have done that harm they've done, so they can make sure it doesn't happen again? If an abuser wants to find help, to learn from someone who knows how to teach them how to protect themselves from becoming a repeat offender, to whom do we tell them they might turn?

We must come to believe that rape sometimes happens to ordinary people under ordinary circumstances. It's so frightening to speak of, the victim might not have even spoken up, so the perpetrator might not even be aware of how much pain they have caused. Once they understand and can name what it is they did and what they themselves have become, they may realize that they want to and are able to change.

Can we see it in their face?

Power Button

I had been asleep for maybe two hours when my cellphone blasted in my face a shrill warning: a child was in danger.

I don't do my best problem-solving when woken from a sound sleep.

I pushed the side button on my phone, and the alarm stopped. But, it took a while for my husband to get up, get his phone from the kitchen, and make his shrieking instrument go back to sleep.

I fiddled with my phone and found two toggle switches. Nighty, night, "Amber Alert" and "National Emergency"!

I felt sorry for all the future Ambers, whose mothers would have to worry about their children in "imminent danger" without my help.

Our government's system to alert us to our own imminent danger? How easy it is, to get a whole nation to shut it down voluntarily.

Decent citizens really want to help the world and its Ambers, but only after they've had a good night's sleep and their coffee.

Pulling Out of Line

The day I found I was not like the other kids, all pushing to get to the top of the sliding board, I pulled out of line and pushed my way back down the metal steps. I knew I did not want to be standing up there on the platform, exulting that it was my turn next, to get to slide down. Others were impatiently waiting for their two-second thrill. Standing in tiers on the ladder stairs, holding onto the railings, they eyed enviously whoever was up top, and yelled impatiently, "Hurry up! We all want to go!" They got back in line, over and over again.

Other kids really, really wanted to slide down the sliding board. So, I got out of line and let them go. I never slid again.

I looked around the playground for something to do, and found her there, playing alone, twirling under the oak tree, The Girl Who Eats Acorns. I asked her why. "Why do you eat acorns?" I did not like her answer. I knew, I did not want to be like her, alone, ostracized, eating bitter acorns, pretending they were yummy, chuckling gloomily at my own performance in theatrical invention.

Impatient for something to happen, to fill the hours of my life, the next day, I did not wait for dawn to unfold. Drawn by the sound of the mourning dove, I ventured forth outside into the twilight of early morning, all by myself, without family or friends or sun.

I found myself at home, warmed at the hearth of song and enlivened by forest fragrance. I was awake, with something fun to do. A new world to explore. There were branches, reaching upwards towards the moon and stars. There were invisible birds, cooing softly, somewhere nearby.

In the distance, there were mysteries, as yet to be unraveled.

Puppy Love

His mom discovered him after school with his new secret love deep inside him. They were in his bedroom. His mom never suspected a thing. This young boy had a love so strong it killed him. It coursed through his veins, though he never wrote a poem or showed anyone anything.

Now, his mother gazed at the two, inseparable in the coffin. They seemed such an unlikely couple, yet they could not be apart, not even in death. They would be buried together.

The community grieved. At the funeral, they shared their memories. The thirteen-year-old honor student. Boy Scout. Big brother to his adoring five-year-old sister. Swim team champion. Best friend of his golden retriever, Scout. Happy-go-lucky kid with the brand-new bike. Always with a smile on his face. The kid with the comic book collection everyone wanted to borrow, and he shared.

At the support group, much later, his mom bravely told her story.

"He was just home from school, not five minutes. I heard him come in. I was in the basement. I called up the stairs, 'How's the weather out there?' He replied, 'Freezing!' and he added, 'Don't bother me, I'm doing homework,' as usual. I heard the door to his bedroom shut. I folded the laundry, came upstairs with the basket, and saw his backpack on the floor by the front door. The apple slices and peanut butter were still on the plate on the kitchen table. I went out and got the mail. His new magazine had arrived, 'Boy's Life,' from the Boy Scouts. He loved the jokes, and he always read them to me aloud. I opened the door to his room to give him his 'Boy's Life,' just to see him smile, and found my son dead on his bed with his new love deep inside him, his heart stolen, his breath taken away, his short life claimed by heroin."

Recovery From Viral Illness Can Be Scary, But Try To Stay Positive

If you do get sick from a viral illness, you can quarantine yourself, take care of yourself, and do what you can to help yourself recover. Don't worry if you are not able to get a test to find out which virus you have. There might not be enough tests when you are sick, or the particular bug you have might be new.

What can you do?

Seek medical advice. No matter how old you are or what underlying conditions you have, you can have a positive attitude while you also rest, drink fluids, and focus on doing what you can to help yourself get better.

When I was twenty-three, I was sick with cytomegalovirus. I was in the hospital three days before they figured out what was wrong with me. I had a very high fever, extreme fatigue, chills, sweating, and severe headache. My liver was swollen. They took blood for testing every three hours around the clock until the doctor announced the news: we now know what's making you sick. The bad news is, there's no medical treatment or cure.

Wait, what?!

It's up to you, the doctor said, to treat this as any other virus. Stay in bed to rest and stay well hydrated. Allow time for your immune system to make yourself well so you don't die. And then, you will have to rehabilitate yourself. Start by getting up out of bed and sitting up in the chair as much as possible, so you don't develop a secondary complication like pneumonia. Start walking when you can. Don't overdo it, or you may relapse. Until you are all healed, don't give up.

I was twenty-three and my whole life jumped into focus. I had the power to heal myself or die? The doctor couldn't do anything for me? What did it mean, to "rehabilitate yourself"? I'd never even heard of rehabilitation.

Sick as I was, I got to work. In less than a week, I had worked myself up to where I could get out of bed and into the chair to sit up, at which point the doctor sent me home, to open up the hospital bed for the next patient. I spent two months on the couch in my mother's living room, mostly alone while everybody else was at work and school. I was lucky it was not contagious, so my family could care for me without themselves getting sick.

I realize now how much PTSD I have from that terrible virus, which did not leave me with any lasting physical damage. It was unbelievably frightening. But I learned a lot about viral illness.

While I was sick, it was overwhelming to be in such pain for so long. But, to be diagnosed, back then, forty years ago, with "FUO" (Fever of Unknown Origin) in a small rural hospital, filled me with fear and excruciating dread, above and beyond the symptoms.

I didn't even know that people my age could become seriously ill, much less of something they could die of, and to have no one know what I had was terrifying. I was sure the torture would last forever.

I had never before seen the view from a hospital bed.

My parents both had full-time and part-time jobs and I was the oldest of their eight kids, so there was no one to sit with me and hold my hand to help me through this ordeal. The young doctor was a friend of my parents, as one of his daughters was in the same class in school as one of my sisters, but I didn't know him. It wasn't until years later I heard the details of how he came to the diagnosis.

In those days before the internet, the doctor, who had just started his own practice not long before, put in hours and hours of time for days and days, laboriously paging through borrowed medical journals, calling colleagues and their extended contacts—dialing on a rotary phone, the numbers handwritten in his notebook before the Rolodex was invented—hunting for clues as to what he should be testing for, and then, for how to treat it.

No one he talked to had any idea of what I had. Mostly recent medical school graduates themselves, they were afraid to guess at how to treat me until they knew what was making me so ill, because they could have made my condition worse. They were even afraid to draw too much blood at one time for the tests. Back then, there was not even hospice, if it came to that—at the time, Karen Ann Quinlan was in a coma, but her parents had not yet won the right for her, or anyone else, to be treated with dignity and compassion if they were at the end of their lives.

It took weeks and weeks for me to be up and walking again for any distance. I had lost all my strength, and back then there was no such thing as physical therapy, and so I lost my part-time job at the bakery I had just started, the best job I could get as a new college graduate with a psychology degree, no real work history, no professional contacts, no resumé, no car, and no social skills.

With me having no insurance and both my parents on teachers' salaries, with a house full of children all coming up to college age, both the doctor and the hospital waived their bills. I still participate in the hospital's fundraisers and donate my giveaways to their auxiliary shop and rummage sales. Medicare-For-All, anyone?

I hear the symptoms of coronavirus and, comparatively, unless I'd have trouble breathing and need a respirator, it sounds like a walk in the park, though I shouldn't make light of it. It is great to know for sure that I'd have some possibility of fighting it off and living through it. And I'd have drugs to hasten my recovery, or at least to help alleviate some of my discomfort.

Today, I could self-diagnose coronavirus quickly based on the symptoms, and I'd be happy to know that I was not alone in my suffering.

And it would be nice to know the name of what it was I was dying from.

Requiem for Petey, The Parakeet

My downstairs neighbor called me. She had just gone shopping.

Her new pet parakeet, Petey, was outside in his cage on her back deck. I could come over later to meet Petey, but first she had to check the messages on her answering machine.

Through my back window, I could hear Petey singing.

My downstairs neighbor called me again. Her mother had called. Her father had had a heart attack.

She flew to Chicago.

After her father's funeral, she returned.

Her anguished scream, "Petey!" flew to my window.

Revenge, Served Cold

The Osage were a poetic Native American tribe whose practices included reciting the creation story, the entire history of the universe, to each newborn baby.

Named after the people of this tribe, who the settlers had denigrated as "savages," the Osage-orange is a hardy tree, but one that is rarely planted anymore. The wood is hard, strong enough for railway ties, and not easily destroyed by forest fires nor nibbling ruminants. The seeds were spread throughout the land by prehistoric beasts tough enough to brave the thorny branches and large enough to swallow whole the fruit, an enormous globule, and trek for miles and miles before pooping out the seeds onto another fertile plain.

Once sewn into hedgerows, today the benefits to property owners are not worth the pain of upkeep. The sticky, sappy insides of the Osage-orange fruits are a homeowner's worst nightmare, gumming up and stalling lawnmower blades, albeit the intention would be to chop them up for easy disposal. Trying to pick up the poisonous monsters by hand is an even worse idea.

As a kid, I played with Osage-oranges large as softballs. They grew abundantly in the strip of wild separating my house from my best friend's, an area where we were forbidden to play but did anyway, climbing the trees, around which were twined poison ivy vines, the spiritual twin of the Osage-orange.

I was awed by the older girl's stories that these grossly pimpled, greenish blobs were heavy-laden, burdened with an ancient Indian curse, and planted by the Osage on purpose to stymie settlers who had stolen their lands.

We had no idea the Osage-orange was the source of our vicious rashes. We believed we were victims of poison ivy.

We culled Osage-oranges as toys, split open the ripe balls, and discovered the wrath of the lingering spirits of the dispossessed, itching for revenge. Their punishments extended even unto us, generations removed and but distantly related to the

European transgressors who had   trespassed their peaceful territory, demolished previously productive communities, terrorized and decimated the indigenous peoples, wiped out their native traditions, beliefs, and customs, and smashed through the boundaries of human decency without remorse and without repentance.

Robot Wars

I was collecting opened soda cans and melting popsicles from the basement after the kids went upstairs, when I heard a vacuous voice. It stated clearly,

"Turn me off."

I never knew that the new doll in town, my daughter's talking birthday gift from a friend, was smart enough to know it needed to save its own battery life and was not too proud to ask a human for help.

"Turn me off."

This human was too busy with her daughter's birthday party to "Read the Fucking Manual," the little paper booklet that came in the box with the toy; not before all the guests had gone home with their goodie bags.

"Turn me off."

Alone in the basement, I was frightened at the sentient sound, knowing no other mind was present, but mine. And, no matter how distinct the taped voice, I could not make out what it was saying. The words were unintelligible. They did not come from a body I could pin with an identity. Unable to comprehend its message, it was impossible for me to comply with its reasonable request.

"Turn me off."

I could not find the source. I was clueless as to the origin of the intermittent, soft syllables. They kept coming, without mercy. I became fearful of looking for it, terrified of what I might find. It sounded like a person calling for help in a faint voice. Was it a child, one of the party guests, still playing hide-and-seek after being abandoned when the party-goers ran upstairs, before finding her? Could it be a full-grown stranger, also playing the game, and calling from a hiding place to a room now empty of its six-year-old girls?

"Turn me off."

Who could it be, hidden in my basement, speaking with so cold, so heartless, an affect? Why couldn't I find them; and where could they possibly be hiding? I could find no one there, though I circled the room and looked everywhere. Was it a person? Perhaps a trapped animal? What do raccoons sound like, when they are injured? Maybe it was a mouse. A cat?

"Turn me off."

When I finally got up the courage, I went around and opened every box, one by one, and dumped their contents out on the floor. I was searching, wandering among the possessions of a small family's lifetime; and waiting to hear it again, hoping to pin down the location from which the mysterious chant was being broadcast. Every space large enough to hold a person was already filled: with toys and out-of-season clothes in boxes; with books not yet unpacked from our recent move; with our stuff.

"Turn me off."

It had to be an animal. I walked, back and forth, the length of the floor. Then I circled around every box again, peeked behind the furnace. I swept my hands over the tops of the bookshelves. There was one small closet door. I opened it, and there stood the large, oval, solitary water storage tank. It was standing upright, made of metal, bright blue. And silent.

"Turn me off."

Right at my feet, I discovered the voice was coming from a large, electronic doll. At least, now, I was face to face with the suspect. The eeriness that broke the silence emanated from within that fake skin, the plastic shell. The doll was reciting a recorded mantra, installed on the factory floor. Though I had listened carefully, I still couldn't make out what it said. I kept listening, and timed it. Three minutes apart. Yet, I still could not comprehend what the words were. No lips moved, to give me a clue. And, for a doll to speak at all—without a child right there, playing with it—that made no sense to me. What made it keep talking? I picked it up and examined it carefully, turning it over and over, searching for anything to explain what was going on. Unlike Chatty Cathy, there was no pull string.

"Turn me off."

It had startled me again. I tried to take it apart. Under its dress, I found the hidden battery compartment, and, finally, I understood. I was hesitant to obey. I did not want to keep touching it, creepy thing. But I had to keep feeling around on the surface of its skin under its dress—and it took me a while before I finally found its recessed on/off switch. I pushed the flesh-colored knob. I decided I did not want my daughter playing with such a vile object, one that would speak whatever words someone in a corporate environment had decided could be shared with little girls. The faceless engineers were one step removed from being physically present, and were not here in person while my children were playing, but I was sure corporate minds would not care to listen to the real little girls and boys, like their mother would. Business suits would not be encouraging little people to speak their own minds. Nor would they be purposefully creative in thinking up responses to whatever of my daughter's thoughts would come from her mouth while playing, making believe she was having a conversation with a real person. Business suits would not listen to my child, wouldn't even think to get to know her well, but somehow they have felt free to feed her lines anyway. Were they hoping she'd bite and find their interaction fun and tell her mom to buy her more dolls? All a marketing executive needed was a way to sell more dolls.

"Turn me off."

What lines were they feeding my daughter anyway? I wanted a permanent solution. I did not have a tiny screwdriver to take out the battery, but I wondered how long it would be, if I turned it back on and simply left it alone, until it failed. Would it continue to repeat, over and over, every three minutes like clockwork, its one insistent demand? How long before the crazed thing would cease its unimaginative play, its repetition of its futile, sterile statement? I carried it upstairs, hiding it under my sweater. I stepped around the Twister game in progress on the living room rug and snuck out the side door and into the garage. I turned it back on. And waited.

"Turn me off."

I wrapped the doll in an old beach towel to muffle the sound and buried it in a cardboard box at the bottom of our trashcan, where it would stay put until garbage day and be put out with the other things we no longer had use for. Left to its own mechanical devices, the batteries would be the first to die.

This was my first skirmish in the Robot Wars, but a Pyrrhic victory. Computers are everywhere now, and I can't trust them. I hate being told what to do by something I can't understand and cannot argue with.

But the worst is when you can't even find the computer you are fighting.

Ruckus

The demand made of my father by Alzheimer's, that he relinquish his treasured love of reading, led to a grotesque frustration ruckus. The book in his hands was still readable.

Oh, but for this demon disease!

In vain, he screamed and he cried for the words to be released. Unable to bear the tease, with brute force he rent the massive paperback he'd failed to complete. In his two clenched fists, he clung to what remained of the tortured tome. He shook and shook and shook the pieces.

He waved and waved and waved his arms above his shoulders, until he was lifted. Raised, a bird in flight; he raced around the room. Dancing on his toes, bobbing and weaving, feinting. A shadow boxer, warming up for his fight.

His underlying illness, lymphoma, did not allow for such exertions as the man would have made in his prime. His futile protestations, fruitless gestures to the gods, and relentless, wracking sobs left him exhausted. But, he did not stop in his active struggling until the charm of music abruptly interrupted.

The mantle clock began its chime. He ceased in pressing his petition. A chapter's worth of pages lay crumpled at his feet. He slumped to the floor, in defeat. Yet, he refused to let go of his grip on the two sectors—the beginning and the end of the story. Though the words remained tantalizingly out of reach, each section, in its partition, held its pages fast, its secrets safe.

Two detached segments of broken spine: this book. This beloved book, its title hidden, huddled in the mysterious invisibility cloak of written, writhing words. This sorry, stolen book: his last.

Samsa's Next Move

The only thing that made his mother think that the metamorphosed monster Samsa had become was not just another beetle, but was indeed her son, waiting for her, next to the steps just outside their front door, was his enormous size. No other insect she had ever seen was quite as large as the hard-shelled vermin that kept its lonely vigil near her home.

And, it wouldn't leave. Her husband, on his way to work each day, would reach the bottom of the brick stairs, check to see if the beast was still there, and frown. His visage turned to a scowl. He'd kick the massive bug out of the bushes and away from their humble, tumble-down cottage, and down the slope of the front yard, past the maple and the oak, and out into the street. He'd turn on his heel, adjust the brim of his hat, and, snarling and cursing under his breath, continue on his way to his office and his government job, now in a foul mood.

No sooner had he seen his father disappear into the hustling stream—the throng destined to die unfulfilled at their desks; and some others who'd also been detained, now late for appointments—the horrid, shiny creature would scurry back to its station beside the porch and hide itself again between the two azaleas. It would continue its solitary watchfulness for his mother's appearance—with a load of laundry or a bushel of apples—and tiptoe up to brush against her ankle as she passed: to remind her of his love, his unending filial attachment.

She looked forward to their encounters and began leaving out for him eggshells and banana peels and the rotten spots cut from cabbages, enough to sustain him so he would not have to wander far in his search for nourishment. Far, to where he might possibly lose his bearings and not find his way back to his spot. No one would have been able to understand him, had he had to stop and ask for directions.

Seckel Pear

The Seckel pear tree was just small enough, I could gingerly set aside my fear of heights and climb up to my perch, jam my sneaker into the crook of a branch, and settle in like a robin placing the first twig into just the right nook, anchored, to start its nest.

I pulled an almost ripe pear until it was freed, and left the leaves and branches shaking. I pared a stiff, green belt from the pear's equator in one eager, slow gnaw, slipping from the pear's waist the slender twirl of a peel, leathery, but scented, so tart, its release, alluring as a feather boa slipped from around the neck of a stripper at the beginning of her act.

The bodacious snap of my buck teeth (prior to my two years of braces) through the peel and into the bulbous base of the fruit made a white gap in the green rind. Removed from the curvy orb, it left a melon-baller-deep, round, aromatic well. The juice did not ooze, but crept from the surface of its breached wall. My tongue did not hesitate, nor waste a lick. The pear's hard, white flesh was lasting, meant for sucking a long time. Its tartness took forever to fade.

The edges of the skin were slow to cede their sting. Not wanting to swallow, not just yet, I wouldn't even chew it like gum, but savored the unyielding firmness between my teeth, nestled between my top and bottom incisors.

I held tight onto the bite, precious as the gleaming gold doubloon from a pirate's chest, the blue bit of eggshell fallen from the robins' nest, the kitten on leave from its mother's breast. I savored and savored the flavor, the autumn harvest to rival Eden's apple, proper ransom for a lifetime's knowledge of good and evil.

I needed to hold forever the pear flavor. The autumn treat was a bit hard to mash, giving so little, inflexible until it had warmed in the mouth for ten minutes. Or, was it merely two? Now, forty-five years later, the passage of time has lost some of its surety.

My molars ground the rough pear, wore down the fibrous pulp slowly, so as to enjoy the grainy gem longer without having to gnaw again more of the hard, unfeeling skin that rasps the gums. My mouth, not used to playing for such high stakes, willingly wagered a rip for the promise of a sip of ambrosia.

My self-serve Seckel pear tree café, perfect for early fall refreshment, stirred a lifetime of wanting to climb back into the nest, to hold again a bit of paradise between two buck teeth on top and two buck teeth on the bottom.

I've been young enough to climb a tree to heaven at an age when I'd never even seen a mirror that let me in on the secret that I had buck teeth, that there was anything less than perfection in life at all.

Snow Balls

Mom always said the perfect toy lay just under our boots. Snow!

Scarves and carrots and coal for the eyes—I just had to step inside a sec to fetch whatever we needed. Each of my kids could make their own perfect snowman. I made sure we had, at the ready, enough twigs for snowman arms, complete with fingers; four pipes—though no one even smokes a pipe anymore; What you have to go through to find a pipe these days!—and hot chocolate with mini-marshmallows. Our favorite mugs waited next to the fire in the fireplace. Warm toes and toasty warm thoughts.

How things changed from when I was a girl. As Olympic skaters on TV triple-axled, I had managed a wobbly "Figure 8" on our pond in my mother's skates. I was twelve. I'd done it. I was done. No more winter for me. I hated the cold weather. I had to wear bobby socks and short skirts to school and never could find two mittens at the same time. Someone else always had my snow pants on when it was time to go out the door. My coat from last year still fit, but the wind reached in at my wrists. My pants were just long enough to cover the tops of my boots—still, some snow would get in. We had no money for fancy sweaters or matching hats and scarves like the neighbor girls with only two kids in their family instead of eight like ours. I did not even know what it meant to "turn up the thermostat." I spent winters curled up with books and our cat. I prayed for spring to skip out on us so July could jump in straight away and I could thaw. I never minded a ninety-degree day—at least I could feel my fingers.

I grew up on peanut butter and jelly and Volkswagens that seat ten uncomfortably. But when I finally grew up all the way, I determined I wasn't going to be crazy like my mom and have eight kids. I was only going to have five, so we could all have clothes that fit and our own beds and boots and mittens.

And opportunities! I scrimped and saved so my baby boy would be able to ski the slopes like an Olympian. Already the fastest runner in his class, my kid was more than an athlete, he was brilliant and fun and good. I wanted him to have all the advantages I'd missed out on. Hot meals and warm baths. Space for things he wanted to do. The latest in cold weather gear and ski lessons I'd never even dreamed how a family could afford. Season passes at our local ski resort. After-school ski club on a bus with the other winter-happy kids and chaperones.

A chance to shine at winter athletics. Sports, his forte, my boy was strong and beautiful and had a smile that made his classmates forget about the handsome ski bum giving lessons. My son would have every chance I'd been denied. I was so proud I'd worked to make this happen for my kids. Everything I'd never had, at their fingertips.

But even so, Santa went absolutely nuts one year. Four hundred dollars in ski equipment for my sixth-grader.

I imagined him, sailing down the mountain, schussing the slopes, swooping up and flying like an eagle. Free to fly. The cold mountain air. The effortless glide to the finish line. Olympic ski champion.

Champion of himself. Champion to me.

Arrangements were made to carpool to the lodge on weekends. I nervously went at midnight to pick him up from his first ski trip. I was anxious to hear him—I was already glowing in the dark.

His first ski lesson. What wind felt like.

How it is—to fly!

The bus pulled up in front of the school and the kids poured out, chattering excitedly.

My son got in the car, quietly. He didn't have his new ski equipment. He'd lost it, on day one.

Sorry, I know it was expensive.
... Nope, don't spend the money.
... It's ok, Mom, I really didn't want to ski anyway.

My heart was broken. His equipment was stolen. He knew we couldn't afford to buy more, so he wouldn't even ask.

Twenty years later, I heard him confess to his cousin.

Nope, I don't ski.
... I've never been skiing.
... No, really, not even once ... I've never wanted to.

Truth is...,

... I've always been scared to death of falling down.

Spatter

Staring at my empty hand, I want your hand to appear, to sprout from my palm as a magic rose, to blossom and grow, envelop my hand from the inside out, surround my hand, my arm, my whole body, to protect me from your having left me to love someone else.

Fighting the force of my longing to go back to "us," I stared so hard at the clock, the hands run backward, then become unhinged from their center joint. They spin wildly about the clock face. The ring holding them down breaks. They fly off into space.

My anger demands ownership of all the air in the room. In the intensity of the vacuum, I can't breathe. Swallowing my heartache sets off inside me an atomic bomb.

My blood runs so hot through my popping veins it melts the crook of my elbow and burns a hole in my skin. Blood seeps out, trickles down my arm. I start to spatter, like bacon in hot grease. I catch fire. My clothes, my hair, everything around me is in flames. My love for you burns hotter and hotter. I am the Large Hadron Collider smashing particles of gold. The ground under my feet melts. I twirl; I'm swirling, lava.

To survive, I will need to drench myself in absolute zero. I flail my arms and run in circles, looking for you.

I find you in my memories: once, on fire; now, a raging snowstorm. A hard, familiar cool emanates from your shell. The coldness of your last words to me grips my arm, their echo shreds my hopes for our reunion. The icy blast I cannot fight against preserves your distance. Your vacant smile hangs mid-air, Antarctica's Cheshire Cat. Your teeth, a string of icicles shimmering in the sun, a jagged line glistening under your thin moustache. The points dangle below your quivering upper lip: tinkling wind chimes from the far side of a frozen lake.

You have nothing more to say.

I'm now a weird afternoon mist hovering over Death Valley. Rattlesnakes scatter, their resting rocks no longer warm. I take your head in my hands and steal a single kiss.

My fire is quenched, my love extinguished. I'm saved from my own blistering wrath, released from the biting sleet of the memory of your touch. I'm no longer tortured.

Now, when I see a hair in my bathroom sink, I still feel a melt in my groin. Your eyelashes started an arduous trek, brushed my cheek, mapped my mysteries, but moved on. I'm freed from insisting you come on the return trip of my life. We had promised each other an eternity. I bought two one-way tickets to paradise on our first date, but my mind has recovered and I'm almost reborn. Another day, I will love again.

When I look up, I see the skies are blue. They are no longer hidden behind endless puff pastry tarts filled with melted smoky Gouda. Through the fluffiness of the white clouds—the duckies, bunnies, and ponies of my childhood—I see mountains in the distance. Green woods, inviting. I feel the endless longing. I hear the calling of a mourning dove for a mate.

Will I love for the first time again?

No, I will love for the first time, for the first time.

Statement From the Pope Needed ASAP

I knew my body, and I knew there were no longer any "I'm a baby, I'm here!" hormones being produced. I knew, from day two—I had miscarried. And so I wanted the failed products of conception removed immediately before they had a chance to harm me.

My doctor refused to believe his eyes when he saw no fetus on the ultrasound at two weeks. One hormonal signal was so strong in my blood, it might indicate life. But there was just one positive result, in all of those many chemical signals he tested for.

No fetus showed on the ultrasound at four weeks. None at six weeks. No change at eight weeks. At ten weeks. At twelve weeks. Everything had died but a small bit of rogue tissue, which continued to send out that one false hormonal reading. The doctor's paperwork kept telling him there was a slight possibility a baby was still hiding in there. It convinced him he should keep waiting, keep searching.

I did not want to wait for the rogue tissue bits to die and stop sending those readings that said, "Maybe there's still a baby, maybe, maybe a baby"—I knew. No, I did not want to wait until what was left in there began to rot. The dead tissue, if not removed, might scar me—or even kill me.

When I asked to speak with someone higher in the management hierarchy of the hospital, he referred me to a colleague at the hospital down the street. She was okay with "performing abortions." He would not perform a D&C to save a woman's life, not if there was a chance there was a baby in there he just hadn't found yet. And he had the final say in determining whether a D&C could be performed at his hospital, a large city hospital named for a Catholic saint.

When the products of conception were finally removed, the surgeon reported they were so scant as to be nearly undetectable.

God gave individuals hearts and minds. Yes, encourage people to pray for divine guidance. But, let a woman and her doctor discuss—facts—during her term of pregnancy.

Let the woman decide the terms of its resolution.

Successful Rape Prosecution Is Uncommon

A week before my eighteenth birthday, I was raped by a casual acquaintance on a school day in the middle of the afternoon. Call me naïve, but it had never occurred to me that a reasonable, nice boy would want to have sex with a girl he'd barely met. And it never occurred to me that a reasonable, nice boy wouldn't take "No, thank you" for an answer. I did not know rape was a thing that happened to ordinary people under ordinary circumstances.

I really didn't know what rape was.

I tried to tell him to stop, to stop undressing me, to get off me, then, desperately, I tried to think of what more I could say to make him understand. I tried, "You don't know what you're doing."

I did not have the language for rape.

I thought I had once read the word "r a p e," but I could not recall where. In an article, somewhere. I had not read the rest of the article, as I only ever read what applies to me. I'd gathered a vague idea of the context, something about sex, so I'd skipped it. I'd had sex already. But "r a p e" was something about strangers, too, I think. Vaguely, about crime. I would not have sex with a stranger, and I do not associate with any bad people, much less criminals. This subject, "r a p e," was of no interest to me because it could not have had any practical application in my life. It was a weird and creepy concept, something I could safely ignore.

Yet here was this twenty-one-year-old boy I had met once, years before, when he was a fellow student in my homeroom when I was a high school freshman, and I was not really sure that this was what they were talking about when they used the word "r a p e" in the article.

I had never heard the word "r a p e" pronounced. How do you pronounce "rape"? Is the "e" silent, the kind of "e" used at the end of a word to give a vowel a "long" sound? Is it "rape," a single syllable with a long "a"? Or, is it a long, drawn-out word, "raaaape," to hint at its danger and the need to beware, to be prepared to run. Is it short and curt, with "rape" said quickly, with distaste, to get it over with, and rid of the taste of the word in the mouth? Or, is it a foreign word of two syllables, a short "a" and a short "e"? "Rah, peh"? Is there a French accent over the "e"? Does one roll the "r," stuttering it over the tongue, hoping to prevent the rest of the word's escape?

What is its root, its etymology? Is it Romantic? Glorified in other countries? Is it Italian? Where in the world did this callous disregard for women originate? Is there a specifically American word for this? Why had I never heard it pronounced? How could I say something aloud to discuss with this boy what I wanted him to stop doing, when I didn't know what to call it?

And, did *he* have a word for it? If he did, it was probably a swear word. Even my best friend never shared the meaning of swear words with me, saying I was too innocent. She didn't want to be the one to corrupt me.

Already, I was all but speechless for terror at what he was doing, so recklessly, with such callous disregard for the person he was touching. I wanted to inform him that he was not participating in consensual sex, yet ... I had no concept that non-consensual sex was a thing, a thing that could be named.

I knew there must be sentences to point out the obvious, like, "You're touching me for your own pleasure, but without my participation." Somehow that phraseology seemed insufficiently inspirational. I did not think hearing it would cause him to change his behavior.

I wanted to feel certain that, if he knew, specifically, that I was not an active and willing participant in this "sex," he would stop. I wanted to say, "I know you would never be doing this if you knew how I am feeling about this." I felt sure he thought I was a friend and would not want to offend me. I wanted to say, "I think you are drunk and acting selfishly. Sober up for just a second so you can see that I want you to stop touching me."

I was a shy, soft-spoken person to begin with who often had trouble in finding the right words to make conversation, and I didn't know what to say. I wanted him to stop touching me, but I did not want to hurt his feelings.

I wanted to tell him, "You don't know that what you are doing to me is something I do not want you to be doing to me, so please stop doing it immediately."

What I actually said was, "You don't know what you're doing."

The way he took offense at what I said, how quickly he got angry and said harshly, "I know what I'm doing!' made me think, he must have thought I was impugning his masculinity, telling him I thought he was not doing "sex" correctly. Somehow judging him on his technique.

He obviously thought it was ok to do "sex" with me. He never considered whether I would disagree with his assessment of my willingness and probably believed I approved of his ravishing attentions.

It seemed it did not occur to him that I might have a differing opinion, that I would think it was not okay to have sex, given these circumstances.

What were "these circumstances" I was trying to explain?

His curt reply was merely meant to reassure me—he was not a virgin. He had done "sex" before, and enough times to know he was doing it right. He obviously had no idea that what he was doing to me was "rape," a crime punishable by years in prison.

He got up and left the room.

I was relieved when he stopped. Despite my lack of adequate language, what I said had made him understand that this sexual experience was not consensual. My speaking up had had the desired effect of getting him to understand that I wanted him to stop. And, he did.

But, when he came back from the bathroom, he brought with him a condom.

I had never seen a condom before, but he waved it in my face, as if to show me, "See? I know what I'm doing." He put it on, then started right in again, this time silencing me by covering my mouth entirely with his mouth, holding my face tight with his head, pushing against my head with his own. The back of my head was smashed against the pillow; the front, entirely under the control of this muscular man.

I fought to breathe, wondering how long it would take to die of suffocation. It truly seemed he had no idea he might kill me through this action.

He flattened my entire body with his strength. He was a champion high school wrestler. He pressed me flat into the mattress and did not let me up. Declared victor by my continued silence, he would still not concede it was the end of the match.

When he finished, he let go of my mouth and raised his head. He covered my entire lower face with his massive hand.

"Shush, my mother is in her wheelchair in the next room. I don't want her to wake up. I'm supposed to be in school."

He was insane, this boy! He had just committed this heinous crime against me, but was more worried that his mother was going to punish him—for truancy?

I realized I had to make sure he did not think that I thought he had committed a heinous crime, that I might cry to his mother or report him to the police. He might see me as a threat and feel he might have to kill me so I wouldn't talk. I had read my Nancy Drew. He had already nearly smothered me when it seemed his firm intention was to keep me quiet.

I had seen how he had become so easily angered, and realized, now, he was very powerful. And, quite drunk. Worst of all, he was not seeing me as a person, a person with an opinion, a voice, the one who had the last word in deciding what happened to her own body. He was not seeing me as a person who was having difficulty communicating, one he should have patience with, one to whom he would have to listen to harder if he wanted to understand me.

It appeared he did not care if he understood me.

I had never seen this type of person before. It was frightening, terrifying, as if he were a tiger who would simply feed, not having the slightest clue that his victim was another living, breathing being, one who also wanted to live.

He must have been one of those "criminals" I had vaguely heard of, a kind of person I had always intellectually disassociated myself from, the kind of person I could not fathom shared a planet with me.

I wanted to leave, quickly and unobtrusively, so as not to wake his mother. What hell-mother—Who could have raised such a monster?—wouldn't have a gun handy and use it to protect her bairn? I did not want to risk being violently attacked, maimed, or killed. In such an unusual and alien environment as I had found myself, I was convinced everyone's behavior must be unpredictable.

To avoid possibly triggering in him a vicious animal reflex, I tried to guide him into what I hoped we both agreed were "socially acceptable" calm behavior patterns. I let him walk me back to school, behaving as if I were being escorted by a chivalrous male accompanying a woman through a dangerous part of town. I hoped to trigger his "protective" masculine reflex. I did not want him to think I thought there was anything wrong. I was afraid if he thought I saw myself as a "victim," he might just play it out, victimize me to the max, no holds barred.

We had walked pretty far from the center of town to get here to his house, but I didn't know where we were or how to get back to civilization. I never paid attention when I went somewhere. I always trusted the people I was with would not let me get lost.

As we made our way along the sidewalks, I held his hand close and smiled disarmingly, warmly, terrified that, if he smelled fear, he would walk me into a deserted area and kill me. We passed many deserted alleys, vacant buildings, and empty parks.

When we were back at the school, I took some time to talk to him, took great pains to try to make him understand this "sex" thing would not be happening again. Not with me.

I was petrified to think he might believe this "sex" had somehow bonded us, and that he and I were now boyfriend and girlfriend.

I did tell him, gently as I could, that I had not consented to "sex," and that this was not okay.

He seemed to understand, and promised not to do it again. To ask first, next time.

No! I wanted to scream. There won't be a next time!

I quietly but firmly insisted there could be no next time.

He did not seem to understand that I had never expected him to touch me without my consent, much less to do this act, which I considered a physical violation. He seemed to have no idea that I considered that what he had done was something "wrong." And

I was too scared to say even that. How might he react if I spelled it out for him? Would he fear that somehow I might desire to punish him, demand retribution? Rape was illegal, with dire consequences for those convicted of the crime. Might that be enough to make him fear my speaking out, to make him want to harm me more in order to silence me and protect himself?

I lied and said I had a boyfriend.

By the time we parted—by all appearances, amicably—we had agreed we could still be friends.

But, only friends. I'd insisted. I have a boyfriend.

I was petrified to have to lie. I was petrified he might find out I lied about having a boyfriend and believe I was a liar, a bad person. Bad people are considered fair game for others to abuse. I had no way to assure myself that he did not consider me now "available" for him to use as he pleased.

I avoided him entirely after that. I did not even go to my high school graduation, believing he would be there.

What else could I do to make sure I could successfully avoid him?—for forever! Forever, forever after!

There was another boy, one I'd had casual sex with for the first time—and what I'd thought would have been the last time—only the week before the rape, and he was only the second boy I had ever had sex with. He had given me my first marijuana, and it was the first, and what I had thought would be the last time, I ever got high, satisfying my curiosity.

And then, he had given me a massage, also my first. Before I knew it, he was having sex with me. Not that he'd asked. I was angry, but I was too high to do anything to help myself get out of the situation. I was mad at myself that I'd been stupid enough to try drugs with a "friend of a friend" and even more embarrassed that I'd let him give me a massage. Though I had said okay when he'd asked, I didn't even know what a massage was—until he was touching me all over. By the time I'd finally gotten home that night, I was so glad I would never have to see him again, and I vowed to be much more careful in the future.

But, to protect myself against further attentions from the rapist, I had given this boy's name as my "boyfriend." Just in case, I let it be known in public. "I was spoken for." I told everyone that this 25-year-old loser was my boyfriend.

I was desperate. I told no one about the rape.

The loser "boyfriend" found out through the grapevine, and was ecstatically happy to hear that I "liked" him. I had to let him take me to the movies a few times. For appearances, so the rapist wouldn't find out I'd lied.

I even let the loser boyfriend massage me. Touch me, and in the same way as he had the first time. I had to make sure to keep him close, as I had to keep seeing him until I could be sure I was not still in danger from the other guy.

I was finding out just how complicated a sexual assault can make one's life.

After a couple of weeks, school ended and I knew I wouldn't be seeing that rapist anywhere. I finally decided it was safe to tell my new "boyfriend" that I wouldn't be seeing him anymore, either. But, I only found the courage to open up, to tell him about the rape and about my fear of the rapist, when I'd had to explain to him why I had burst into hysterics when we got back from seeing a movie at the theater.

There was a rape scene in the movie. Such a short time before, I had never even been aware of rape, and now, again, there it was, in my face.

Rape was a horrific experience. I would never want anyone else, ever, to be raped.

My new "boyfriend" understood completely when I apologized for how I had been using him for protection from further advances by the rapist.

Then I found out, he himself was the protective type. He felt very protective—of me.

My new "boyfriend" offered to have the rapist killed. For my peace of mind—a guarantee he would not rape me or anyone else. It wouldn't cost too much. He would get the money, somehow. He knew at least three guys from the South Bronx he could've asked, and another one who lived in our town. For the right price, he could convince any number of guys from the city to come here to take care of business.

My "boyfriend" would take care of the expense. He didn't have the cash, but he had a new job. He'd save up. It was just a part-time job pumping gas. It might take a while.

I did not want anyone to be murdered, not even a rapist, not even this one, who I feared still might murder me to keep me from testifying if the police found out and prosecuted the case.

My new "boyfriend" promised to say nothing. To tell no one, ever, that I had been raped. To never confront the rapist.

On learning how easily my "boyfriend" had entertained a casual indulgence with the concept of murder, I immediately "broke up" with him.

But, only in my head. It took me three years to get up the courage to believe I had found a way to get him to let me leave him without my feeling he might decide he needed to have me murdered by a friend from the South Bronx, or even from my own hometown.

For a very long time, it felt like I was living among alien beings from another planet. I had no idea how people could live with such violence. I didn't understand it. I didn't know how to protect myself from it, nor how to permanently distance myself from these people who were so cozy with the concepts of rape and murder. I did not know how to distinguish one of the vicious from among the ordinary people I thought I knew.

In the months following the rape, I spent every free minute with my "boyfriend" in fear for my life, hoping that his reputation for violence—which I'd never known about nor suspected, he was so loving and gentle—would help to protect me from the rapist trying to attack me again. But now, I was worried to death this new form of violence might become manifest against me.

Decades later, a former classmate told me how she had been raped the week before I was, and by the same boy from our school who had raped me, and how she had screamed at him during the rape, and how badly he had beaten her. She had filed a police report immediately. They took pictures of her bruises and swollen face and filed a hospital report, evidence of her contusions and broken bones. They gave her a lie detector test, which they told her she failed. She had said her name, for the record, calmly, and the machine recorded that she had told the truth. She then cried hysterically through every other question. The machine recorded her emotional reaction as "lying."

There was no further investigation.

She, too, had not known him well. She, too, had been invited up to visit him for the first time and to see his new stereo. She, too, had felt a little sorry for the boy who had few friends, no one with whom to share the joy of his new acquisition. She, too, was inexperienced with men. Following her experience with the police, she, too, had told no one else what had happened, holding her silence over twenty years. She had feared for her life.

She was only telling me, now, in the parking lot of the local supermarket, because I had just told her I had just read our classmate's obituary and was relieved to know he was dead. I'd shared my story.

Then she shared hers.

When I heard the heartbreaking details, I was disgusted and furious with our local police department for not pursuing prosecution, which could have protected me, too. At the time, I had no idea I was not his only victim.

How many more? I had no idea anyone else in my school, in my town, or even in the whole world had ever had to suffer what I'd been through.

Rape? I'd never heard of such a thing. I was sure if such a thing had ever happened before, it would have been reported, it would have been in the news. I would have been informed. All girls would have been made aware of the need to protect themselves.

I would have known his name.

I would have known to be careful, and not to think this quiet boy was reaching out to me because he was in need of a friend.

I read his obituary. The man died prematurely at age forty-three, leaving no family, no descendants. Cause of death: unknown.

I couldn't help but wonder whether someone had finally placed a phone call to the South Bronx.

Summer Vacation With SpaghettiOs

My sister and I, on parole from our long and lonely rural road, spent a week every summer in the city with my great-aunt Zaza, who lived all alone with her fear of cats and SpaghettiOs in a can. She believed the TV ads and hoped to see stars in our eyes when she served us the gourmet dinner for spoiled children.

SpaghettiOs tasted so tinny, I could not choke them down. Nor could I staunch poor Zaza's tears. She'd cut back on eating all month to afford us our treat. We were not amused by her zeal. When we asked for dessert, she served vanilla, one scoop. When we asked for a topping, she dribbled green crème de menthe. It was all we could do, to tolerate red lipstick on chapped lips, cement sidewalks, thick eyeglasses, bright-colored dresses, and her enormous expanse of frizzled orange curls, which she tied up in floral scarves when it rained. My sister allowed herself to be drenched in Zaza's fancy cologne. I would have gladly paid my life to be rid of the stench.

Zaza carried capacious purses covered in carpet, lined in silk. They held no candy: nothing but an embroidered lace handkerchief, a comb, a nearly empty address book, the stub of a pencil, a mirrored compact, and a lipstick. My grandmother joined us for morning outings. We forayed into museums, salted pretzels, and Italian ice. Grandfather, his pocket knife, and decorum showed up at noon. Whereas Grandmother and Grandfather wore sensible shoes, Zaza's high heels hurt, which shortened our trips to the Philly Zoo and picnics in the park.

When my cot was pulled out from the closet and unfolded, I was surrounded all night by sounds of the street. The sirens and screams sounded much like cicadas at home. Iron barred the first-floor windows of Zaza's row house in the city, protecting my great-aunt from those street predators she hadn't as yet invited in.

Tall for His Age

The boy is merely a high school freshman, but, tall for his age, he looks older. Years of swim team competitions gave him muscles. His bushy hair reflects that he hasn't had a haircut lately and he has some Semitic heritage on his father's side, back three generations.

He lost his cell phone last week and hasn't yet mown enough lawns to buy a new one, much less pay for a haircut, and his parents are making him tough it out, to learn the hard way how to be a responsible citizen.

And, besides, no one looks at his hair.

His sunburnt skin from swim meets and mowing lawns renders his complexion nearly swarthy. His skin is dotted with acne, which multiplies the basic insecurity he wants to outgrow to please his mother. His not knowing what he wants to be when he grows up is nearly hidden under his math-whiz accomplishments, which his father brags about to his co-workers while pressing his son to keep up the good grades and study hard, stressing he needs to get a scholarship and go to a good college and make his family proud.

The boy is waiting for his mother to pick him up. He is at the county fair, near the exit—he was volunteering, cooking burgers for the Rotary—and she is late.

She is never late. And he is all by himself. And he is never all by himself. Where is his mother?

He is waiting at the exit, just inside the gate, exactly where he is supposed to be. But, before today, he had never been alone, unsupervised, responsible for himself. This is a trial run, his spending an hour on his own at the county fair will help him to discover what it means to be a grown-up, to take care of yourself, to solve your own problems.

He can't call his mom or his dad, because he has no phone. He has never been without his mother near, something she thinks he needs to outgrow. He has video game withdrawal from having no cell phone to play with, which lends him an air of heightened anxiety, multiplying his lost-child fretting over his mother's lateness and his worry he won't get home in time to mow the last lawn before dark.

He looks terribly nervous and upset, eyeing the exit, shifting his feet, left to right and back again. He dare not leave the spot to find the Port-A-Potty in case she arrives to find him irresponsible, not where she expects him to be. He puts down his heavy backpack. He picks it up, he puts it down again. There is nowhere to sit.

His face is not yet shaven, little more than peach fuzz. He's got the hunched shoulders reflecting good, old-fashioned, American-teen sullen, Santa-is-watching paranoia, good-son submissiveness. He's so worried. He keeps a vigilant eye out for her arrival. He can't take out his textbooks to study while he waits, or he might miss her.

But, he is not alone. Strangers at the county fair—a posse of rednecks who have just spent too much time in the beer tent—surround him. They have mistaken this tall, nervous, responsible boy, on the verge of tears for worry over his missing mother, for an adult man of middle-eastern descent, an Islamic terrorist, a nervous would-be suicide bomber. He seems, to them, to portray the perfect visage of nervous religious zealotry—his backpack condemned as likely to be holding a bomb.

A man in a jeans jacket with an American flag patch yells at the boy to go back to his own country, rendering the already upset, frightened boy speechless and terrified. The boy is clueless as to what this intoxicated madman is raving about, but hears in his slurs an unmistakable hostility, clearly directed at him.

The drunken good ol' boys take turns harassing the boy. One man shoves him, and he catches himself without falling. The circle of men unhinge a swarm of metal buckles from their belts, remove the belts from their loops, and start swinging, whipping leather in the boy's direction.

A U.S. Marine in uniform just happens to be buying cotton candy ten feet away and catches sight of the near-hysterical look on the boy's face. He asks the boy if he could use some assistance.

The soldier stays with him until his mother arrives.

Tap Out

Y ou didn't tap out."
    Sensei knew from years of experience he had to stop twisting my arm. The slightest bit more pressure, the next nudge would have snapped the bone.

"Didn't it hurt?"

He could not tell by my face, by my body language, or by the amount of pressure I exerted in self-defense to keep him at bay.

And, I didn't know. I couldn't remember.

I had learned to try to forget pain, to not let hurt show. But now, in studying karate, Sensei told me, to protect myself, I would need to retain a consciousness of my pain. And I would have to tell him when to stop.

No one had ever asked me before if one more push would be too much. No one had ever asked me for my permission before forcing me beyond my level of tolerance, to the unbearable.

Sensei says, I have to learn to trust; that when I tap out, the hurting will stop.

I can't shake the feeling that I need to be stronger than is possible, in order to endure what is inevitable.

I want Sensei to fight me as hard as he can until I break.

I want Sensei to know just how strong I've already had to be—to know—I've been broken, and not only did I survive, but I thrive.

Tastykakes

Never had heaven seemed so close as on church day, when, on the way home, we stopped at the newspaper store full of all the treasures a weekly allowance could buy. When I got a raise in my allowance, enough to buy more than a single candy bar, I discovered Tastykakes.

Tastykakes! Chocolate cake, chocolate frosting, topped with an iced royal coat-of-arms fitting of most exalted status in all treatdom.

Mom never bought Tastykakes.

Dad ate only those treats Mom made, but he let us buy whatever we wanted with our allowance, to learn the value of money. A package of two Tastykakes cost twelve cents. So worth it!

After Dad passed, Mom and I talked of preserving family recipes. I rarely cooked or baked anymore. When I wanted a treat to remind me of my childhood, I bought Tastykakes.

"What was Dad's favorite dessert?" I knew Mom had had more time to bake before she had us eight kids. "Did you ever make Cherries Flambeau?" Dad had often joked after dinner, "Bring on the Cherries Flambeau!" which never materialized. The fanciest I could remember was red Jell-O with floating bits of fruit cup.

Mom let out a sudden roar. "I slaved over those cupcakes!"

When she calmed a bit, she explained.

"When we were first married, I used to bake all the time, but he never appreciated it. One day, I made chocolate cupcakes. I even iced them. I left them on the counter and was going to bring some for my bridge club, and they disappeared! All twelve of them! Then, your father had the nerve to say, 'Elsie, you've perfected the Tastykake!' If he couldn't tell the difference, why should I slave in the kitchen? Let him just buy them in the store!"

She was still livid.

Testifying Before Congress

A poised and most courageous woman, her words came calm and clear on TV. As she told her story, every word rang true. You'd know it, too, if it had happened to you.

Her ordeal was not so unusual. Did she not know that this happens all the time? Did she not know, because nobody—nobody!—nobody ever talks about it?

Was she afraid that if she did not speak up, this terrible man, wielding a gavel of wood, would have the power to compound wrongs? He had treated her dreadfully, then showed no comprehension of her fear. All she wanted was to tell her truth, and let others decide how to proceed.

She thought of the next girl, and she knew that this man, who could be so blind as to what good behavior looks like and what sort of behavior should never be allowed, shouldn't be put in charge of deciding anyone's fate.

The *Beowulf*

The orphan shows her adult son the *Beowulf*.

"A saga. Pop-Pop's favorite."

Her father's bass booms from her son's chest, "I know, Mom. He told me."

The orphan gives another of her mother's nieces the recipe and a jar. Each promises to keep the sourdough alive; each is sorry to have to lie.

As the stock market plunges, the orphan's husband keeps up, on his cell. The family trust dips slightly; it has to take care of his wife's brother.

Who was it who chopped tree trunks all day long every day for two years during the Great Depression to buy enough potatoes to feed the whole family their one, evening, meal?

The Hardest Thing

I wrote a poem about one of my #MeToo moments. The hashtag #MeToo has recently been used on social media as a way to discuss, without going into detail, the fact that a person has experienced sexual assault. Discussing the details of sexual assault is difficult. When you read about one person's #MeToo experience, you maintain an awareness that there remain, unsaid, many similar stories.

Merely becoming aware of the #MeToo hashtag has been difficult for me, as it stirs memories, which, if I may, I will share here, in chronological order. I have been lucky in having few such incidents to recall. Many women are not so lucky.

What is the hardest thing I've had to deal with along the lines of the #MeToo movement?

1
It was not that time when I was thirteen and forcibly French-kissed by the dad of the kids I was babysitting for while his seven kids were in the next room watching TV.

2
It was not when I was seventeen and skipped school to go to a bar with a new friend and accepted his offer to stumble across town with him to sober up at his house before getting on the school bus and he showed me his new stereo in his bedroom and turned the sound up really loud and raped me while his disabled mother was in a wheelchair in the next room and I missed my high school graduation a month later because I couldn't bear the thought he was also going to be there and I also found out he had received an award for his star athletic prowess because he was invaluable to his team.

3

It was not when I was nineteen and at a summer concert in Central Park and my boyfriend struck up a conversation with a friendly group of boys and a girl and then accepted a hit of their marijuana as we sat hidden in a secluded area off the main path through the park and my boyfriend passed out and the seven boys gang-raped me in front of the girl, who sat watching.

4

It was not a month later when I left the movie "Billy Jack," crying over the movie's rape scene, which prompted me to finally tell my boyfriend what had happened in Central Park and he pressed me to tell him over and over all the details and it turned him on and he insisted on sex every few hours over the next two weeks.

5

It was not a month later when I tried to break up with my boyfriend and he assumed the only reason I would ever leave him had to be because I already had another boyfriend and he threatened to kill himself and me too and it took me another two years to figure out how to leave him without him killing me in a jealous rage.

6

It was not when I was twenty-two and needed stitches in my wrist from fighting an acquaintance for the car keys while he was driving after he told me he was not going to drive me home but instead take me to the hotel he and his friend were staying at so they could rape me and I grabbed the wheel and crashed the car into a parking meter and in the struggle I broke off the car's turning signal and the metal shaft sliced a long gash which left a scar which is still noticeable and I have had to explain the story over the years as close friends and relatives have asked about the scar which makes it appear that I might once have tried to slit my own wrists, but only on one arm, and I didn't.

7

It was not when I was twenty-two and strong enough to fight off a 28-year-old date-rapist who admitted to me he had raped a date the night before but did not think it was such a big deal because he had date-raped regularly, almost every night, since he'd started dating at age fifteen and no one, not one of his victims, had ever reported him to the police and I'd been the first one strong enough to fight him off.

8

It was not when I was twenty-two and my date's best friend drove me home from a party because my house was on his way and he stopped the car at the side of the busy state highway and raped me for an hour and left me in a deserted parking lot at a highway rest stop at three in the morning.

9

It was not when I was twenty-two and my boyfriend's friend came with another acquaintance to deliver the news of my boyfriend's suicide and the two raped me without allowing me to get my diaphragm or cream for birth control and my boyfriend's friend told me he wanted me to have his baby to remember his friend by and later when I told him I had had an abortion he told me I should have kept the baby because I could be sure the baby was his because the acquaintance was sterile from a horrific construction accident and couldn't have been the father and I wouldn't have had to worry about raising the baby on my own because he supported his other three kids with $50 monthly payments to the baby mommas and he would have done the same or better for me.

10

It was not when I was twenty-three and my boss regularly forced me to perform sex acts in the office with the door closed while six other employees were within earshot and when I eventually broke down and cried in confidentiality on the shoulder of a co-worker and he reported it to the company owner's wife and rather than deny it the offender simply remained mum and refused to even speak a word on the subject and I had to endure the humiliation of her intense questioning over the course of a week until the offender was fired.

11

It was not when I was twenty-four and had a heart-to-heart with my fiancé and graphically described all the times I had been sexually assaulted and he listened lovingly and I couldn't imagine why all men weren't like him.

12

It was not when I was twenty-five and went to confession the morning before I was about to be married and confessed the abortion knowing I would not be able to be married the next day because abortion was an unforgivable mortal sin and the priest absolved me of the sin and gave me the penance of saying three Hail Marys and I said the penance and in my wedding photos my eyes are puffy from crying so much.

13

It was not when I was twenty-seven and managed to fight off a business client who had arranged to meet me in my office after hours because of his scheduling conflicts and he said he needed to discuss a large purchase which was a lie to get me alone to grope and kiss me in front of the rolling security cameras and he threatened to show the film to my husband and my co-workers.

14

It was not when I was forty and read in the local newspaper the obituary of the guy who had raped me in high school and relived all of my #MeToo moments.

15

It was not the day, ten years after that, when I ran into a dear friend from high school in the parking lot at a local supermarket and we discussed who had died since graduation and I told her I was not sorry when I had, ten years earlier, read the obituary of the high school wrestling star who had raped me and I told her candidly about the rape.

16

It was not the moment after that, when she told me that this same rapist had raped her a week, to the day, before he had raped me.

The hardest thing I've had to deal with along the lines of the #MeToo movement was listening to her describe the aftermath of her rape, which she had immediately reported to the police, who did not believe her. They made her take a lie detector test, and then told her she had failed the test because the results showed that the only question she had answered truthfully was "What is your name?" They sent her home and he remained free to rape me and god knows who else.

Yes, that was the hardest thing, finding out that we do have a system in place to protect us from rape and the system is ignored. That was the hardest of all.

Until something even worse happened, which happened to a loved one, which I cannot even begin to talk about.

And then, something even worse. Another loved one.

And yet, I am whole. I never think of myself as a survivor of sexual assault. It just doesn't define me, and I don't sit around and dwell on it, or even think about it.

This is just one more poem in my sometimes painful, sometimes beautiful, complicated life. It's for the awful things that *didn't* happen to me, that I'm grateful. It could have been so much worse.

It is a fact that sexual assault continues to happen. That is what moves me, what drives this poem. People are hurting, every minute of every day, as a result of sexual assault.

Sexual assault happens. Often. This has to stop, and right now.

Please, do something! Save me from having this happen to me again! Save the next woman. The next boy or girl or man or baby. Yourself. Your sons and daughters. We need to figure this out.

The emotional pain and fear and horror from sexual assault is fathomless and endless.

Imagine:

* You are screaming from inside Jonah's whale, being dragged across the bottom of the ocean, seven fathoms under the surface, with your lungs full of salt water, and the whale's stomach acids are already dissolving your eyeballs, tongue, and bones.

* You are drowning in a sea of needles stabbing you in your eyes, inside your mouth, under your fingernails. You are inhaling needles into your lungs, and needles are piercing every inch of your skin and every point in your body, inside and out.

* There is a tide coming in and you are pinned under a rock in the sand at the edge of the water while crabs are clipping off your private parts and mosquitoes and black flies are feasting on your exposed skin and videographers are showing the live feed of your traumatization online, betting on how long you will survive.

* You are zoned out on your computer or smartphone, playing your favorite video game, passing time because there is nothing else to do while you wait.

Except, no!

This last one is exactly what does happen. Many can't see that sexual assault has anything to do with them. They can't imagine what kind of action they could take that would stop sexual assaults from happening. It is exactly what people do when they think about the best way to deal with rape culture—they ignore it.

Do you, too, feel powerless to change the world? At a loss for ideas on how to make all people respect the right of every individual to determine what is an appropriate way to speak with them about their bodies and to grant them the right to insist on consent for each instance of physical contact?

How do you even make everyone aware of what it is that constitutes sexual misbehavior? Here, I have written a poem outlining my experiences. But how do I get everyone to agree that it is time we all commit to learning about and freeing ourselves from having our bodies used against our will?

The first step is to talk openly about rape. Talk about sexual assault. Talk about what kinds of sexual talk or behavior feel uncomfortable. Talk about what behaviors are unacceptable. Talk about the intolerable things people do to one another's bodies. Talk about what type of physical contact feels torturous.

Support the sea change in attitudes happening now during the #MeToo movement, and don't let the tide ebb on this one. We need a tidal wave, a tsunami of change about how we think of our own and each other's bodies. How we talk can change the ways in which people touch one another. We want to assure that the touching of each other's bodies is always accomplished with mutual compassion and respect.

We need to talk about sexual assault. Men need to hear how much their assaults hurt, so they understand how important it is to take control of their own behavior and end the pain.

I hear women say they do not want to admit to men how much they have been hurt. They'd deny their own pain, to make sure to deny men any possible enjoyment they might feel on finding out that they'd inflicted pain.

The Hardest Thing, Post-Script

At the time of each incident of sexual harassment or sexual assault, I learned something new. I had no idea beforehand that anyone would think to target my body sexually to take it, especially men I considered "ordinary, good guys," who were considered "good" by themselves and the community.

There always are bad people, but what makes people who are ordinarily good think it is okay to help themselves to a woman's body? Women are schooled on how to cope with the trauma of sexual assault. No one seems to know how to prevent ordinary people from sexually assaulting. Rather, what passes for popular entertainment is often a how-to manual on how to assault with guiltless impunity.

There should be more formal study, not on the "crime" of rape, but on how to teach everyone to understand that the integrity of a person's body is sacrosanct. I want to see funding for studies "What Causes a Man to Have a Casual Attitude Towards Rape?" I want studies to find out how an otherwise ordinary, good person can think it is acceptable for them to rape someone. I want major newspapers to run special sections: "How to Prevent Rape in Your Family." I want to see books for new parents, "Successful Strategies for Preventing Your Child From Becoming a Rapist."

At the moment, the problem is not only that there are no answers, but that the conversation is still limited to condemnation of criminal behavior or to whispers of "Me, too."

Bring rape out of the closet. Make it safe to talk openly about rape.

The Shiny Lime Green Gift Bag

Ah, for the olden days. By now, I'd be back to playing mah jongg on my phone. Sitting in my car, waiting for the vet tech to bring me back my dog and my credit card. He'd tell me, "Arliss is such a good boy! So cute! Look at that face. He did fine with his shot. No problems." I'd drive home.

But, no. I'm a poet. So, I am fully aware, recording the moment as it unfolds. I don't want to miss a thing. I want to get it right.

My thumbs pace over the small screen as an expectant father paces the delivery ward hallway: hoping for "perfection"; not sure he'll be willing to settle for "breathing."

A poem is being born.

I'm hoping to capture every word verbatim. Every edit becomes the magic of the photographer's darkroom. But the camera must first be preloaded with high-quality film, the depth-of-field set, measurements taken and adjustments made for the ambient lighting and highlights. The camera is focused, the zoom lens tweaked. One hand and the thumb and four fingers of the other have to balance the weight of the machine. The forefinger poised on the button is ready to capture the candid—the moment it happens—or it is lost.

All of it is important, whatever the poet can sense. Every smell, the poet must identify and sleuth, trace back to its origin. There is a strong smell of dog from Arliss's crate on the back seat of my tiny blue Honda Fit. I make a mental note to throw his car blanket into the laundry when I get home.

Traffic rolls by on this country road, which postures on a billboard with an important-sounding name. The road sign here at the vet has the non-descript label, "State Highway 94," but the ad claims that, a few blocks south, "High Street" is prime real estate for the medical arts.

The average noonday crowd is on its way to pick up Oriental Chicken Salad from Applebees or Kung Pao Chicken from Chun

Bo's. Or, someone is going out on their lunch break to make a deposit while the bank is still open. But, I'm guessing, not observing.

I note the make and model of the cars in the vet's parking lot. An older Corvette Stingray, powder blue with black racing stripes. My car, in my alternate universe.

A women rolls down its window, as I try to see myself in her skin, wearing that 'Vette.

The side door of the vet's building opens, and I see my fluffy-headed little monster spring from the vestibule into the frosty air and take command of the sidewalk.

"He's a spitfire! He was running all over, saying hi to everybody. He's so friendly. And adorable! He ran up and down the hall, and ran circles around everybody's feet."

They give me back my dog, handing me his leash.

He's running in circles. Leaping like a pod of dolphins. I lead him from the office door down the sidewalk and stairs and through the parking lot. He bounds to the car. A bucking bronco, eager for another ride in the car, he knows behind which car door awaits his crate. He dances, hounding me for admittance, a pre-teen in a trainer bra in the lobby at the Ed Sullivan Show, screaming for Ringo.

And the woman who came out that door, just ahead of me— we're here at the vet two weeks before Christmas—leans out of her 'Vette window and says, "Cute dog. He's so happy."

"Thanks," I say. I no longer get angry when perfect strangers compliment me on stuff totally beyond my ability to design—my adorable children, my friendly dog, my hair. Some people love my straight hair and ask me my secret, but I can only admit, I've got nothing to do with it. I just wash it, comb it, and let it dry, and it's always perfect, at least in the eyes of people who wish for straight hair. I want curls, but when I try to curl my hair, even when it's been permed, it goes flat in ten minutes. It always looks the same, no matter what I do. I comb it out when it's wet because otherwise it gets rats'-nest tangled and impossible to tame.

Tame was the name of the cream rinse my mother used on us kids so she could comb our hair after a bath without us screaming in agony. Whenever we ran out of Tame, we'd howl and screech like wild animals losing a jungle fight.

The Breck Girl. That's who I wanted to be. She had perfectly combed, wavy hair. You could tell she never screamed. Her hair never tangled. The Breck Girl's hair products were perfect, at least in the magazine ads.

I don't care what my hair looks like, as long as it doesn't torture me. I only comb it out while it's wet because it hurts so much to try to comb the knots out later.

I don't use hair products, except for creme rinse, nor beauty products. I'm just lucky I can get away with my normal, ordinary appearance. When I used to wear makeup and try to look fashionable, I couldn't walk down the street without strange men calling me "a blonde bombshell" or telling me "Honey, you look like breakfast in bed!" It's not that I really don't care how I look. It's just that I don't need that kind of drama in my life.

But, as much as I try not to draw attention with my looks, I find it interesting to look at other people. Each has hair that's unique and is perfect for them. I try to get to know people, the real person under the costume they wear. What's under the skin? Each has a story. Fiction is fun, but truth is endlessly fascinating.

Now I'm looking more closely at the 'Vette girl, the one who's been sitting in the sports car, and she's looking at me, still smiling at my dog. She's made no indication she's getting ready to leave.

Is my Arliss really that adorable, that total strangers would sit in a parking lot in winter with the window rolled down, just to enjoy his ebullience?

I'm paying attention and writing this down. The 'Vette girl doesn't start her car's engine. She hasn't put on her seat belt. She gets back out of her car and shuts the door. But she doesn't walk toward me and my dog, or toward the building—or at all. She just stands there.

Why is she lingering in the vet's parking lot? It's cold. She's wearing a white woolen coat and carrying a shiny little lime green gift bag, holding it close to her heart.

I wonder if she's on her way to a birthday party. Maybe the birthday party doesn't start until after dinner and she's got some time to kill. What's in the bag? With such an expensive car, she might have bought an expensive gift.

Maybe something with diamonds. They say, good things come in small packages.

Why do I keep making things up? I want facts. I am recording her story in my mind—but what is her truth? There is poetry in this moment, her moment, whatever it is. Beauty. Joy. Drama. I'm paying attention. I want to get it right.

She tells me again how happy Arliss looks. "What a great little dog!"

I don't want to say a thing that might break the spell.

She smiles, and she says, "Mine's in here." She pats the lime green gift bag she's holding to her chest, the plain, small, shiny paper bag she nestles at her breast.

There is no sign of movement from the bag. Is she trying to tell me her dog is taking a nap in that gift bag? Maybe she doesn't have a dog carrier, and only has fancy little bags at home to carry things in, bags she's accumulated over the years, from always only shopping in jewelry stores. Did she bring her dog to the vet in a bag so she can carry it with her into Macy's to do her Christmas shopping on the way home? What kind of a dog is that small? My dog, Arliss, is a shih-tzu, and he's small for a dog, but he would never fit in that bag. What's smaller than a shih-tzu? Is hers a chihuahua? How big are chihuahuas? Maybe its a puppy chihuahua, maybe the runt of the litter. And designer dogs can be very small, specially bred. And they're very expensive; she could afford one. Is it a teacup terrier? A "peki-poo"?

She's paid a fortune for this dog, and this is probably a newborn puppy on its first visit to the vet.

But, that's *my* story. What is *hers*?

She pats the bag again, tugs it more tightly to her chest. There is no sign of movement at all from the little bag. Is she trying to tell me …

I panic, and I think of Frank, at my poetry workshop. Frank's poem said, "my wife's cough—a gunshot—"

I curse my profession—God, whatever made me think I wanted to be a poet?!—and my compulsion to untangle the truth in the hardest way—

To find the poem in each moment.

I wonder, how I am ever going to be able to read the words aloud at a poetry reading?

There is no sign of movement from the little bag. Her fingers clutch its handles. She's looped her hands and wrists through the white cords. I can't read her face, but she clings almost desperately to the package in her hands.

I can't unhear her say the words. "Mine's. In. Here."

My imagination runs wild, and my heart is aching for her.

She pats the silent, still, lime green gift bag.

"Twenty-two years." There's a little catch in her voice.

My frisky little Arliss is only thirteen and is a shih-tzu, a breed that never lives to twenty-two, sixteen at most. Her dog is definitely another small breed. Only the small dogs live that long. To live to twenty-two, she must have taken extraordinarily good care of her pet.

I want to comfort her, to find words to express my condolences. To show her I now understand why she was so attentive to my dog, why she's still here in the parking lot in the cold, still soaking in Arliss's dancing, his joyous prancing around in circles.

I almost ask, "What was your dog's name?" but I find I'm too overcome. I can't even speak.

She pats the bag, and says, "My cat."

Theater Bio

Susanna played a singing, dancing townsperson in her high school's production of the musical *Once Upon a Mattress*. Her first speaking role on the big stage was as Karen in Neil Simon's *Plaza Suite* at the Garris Theater in Branchville, NJ, though it was actually a small stage, a tiny theater-in-the-half-round, where she also appeared the following year in a non-speaking role, playing a juror in *Inherit the Wind*. After a long hiatus from theater, often singing classical music with the Sussex County Oratorio Society, she made her debut with Cornerstone Playhouse in Sussex, NJ, playing the role of Cora in the Noel Coward comedy, *Waiting in the Wings*. The following year, she performed again with Cornerstone, in the musical *Fiddler on the Roof*, playing the ghost of Fruma Sarah.

Susanna's interest in theater goes back further. When she was twelve years old, she wrote and directed a play she produced herself, *The Witch and the Princess*, and [type-] cast her little sister in the role of the Princess, preferring herself to play the role of the Witch, and cast another neighborhood kid in the supporting role of the Wizard. Susanna sold twenty-two tickets at a quarter apiece, and all of the neighborhood kids came out to see the premiere performance and enjoy the homemade chocolate chip cookies and lemonade offered at intermission, served by Susanna at the concessions stand she had constructed. The refreshments had been prepared by Susanna, who had also designed and constructed the costumes and set and created and hung advertising posters to promote the event. Closing after just one night, *The Witch and the Princess* enjoyed rave reviews, written by Susanna. The play had been considered by all in attendance to be the highlight of the summer, since nothing else at all ever happened. Ever.

Literally, nothing. Nothing. Ever. Happened.

Susanna's earliest recollection of her being in possession of a gift for the theatrical is from the summer after she had turned five, just before she began kindergarten. She awoke at dawn every morning to go outside and listen to the mourning doves' cooing, and after finishing her glass of milk she would announce the news of the day to her imaginary television audience.

"Good morning, boys and girls! Yes, it's summer! It is still summer today! So make sure to go outside today and play. Because it's fun! And ... there's nothing else to do! As usual.

"Come outside! See the amazing tall weeds with the yellow flowers! See the tree, still here, just like it was ... yesterday! Come, see all the sights you can see from the front porch ... and from the driveway. Don't worry about the cars on the road, folks, because ... there aren't any! It's very quiet here! But it's fun and exciting! Just like the circus ... only without the elephants and ponies and tigers and trapeze. Exciting! ...even without the hot dogs and cotton candy.

"Well, that's life here in the neighborhood, folks. That's all we have for today. This has been a production of the morning television news, coming to you from the front porch. This news has been brought to you by Chocolate Chips. Chocolate Chips! It doesn't get much better than that, folks! Get some Chocolate Chips today. You'll be glad you did."

There Is Nothing To Be Done

Back in April, I told you kids not to disturb that pair of robins that was building their nest over the porch. I told you, let nature take its course. Now, it's August, and this afternoon, I remembered that as I paused on the porch after mowing the lawn before going inside to turn off the coffee pot. I peeked inside the finished nest. In there, I saw three pale blue eggs. Intact.

I didn't call the other kids or Dad. I took down the nest myself and carried it to the thicket of weeds behind the tree on the farthest edge of the property out back. I dumped the eggs out on the Queen Anne's Lace.

Remember I told you, Queen Anne's Lace is a blossom of many flowerettes, cleverly disguised as one, soft flower? There's lots of Queen Anne's Lace around that tree, and lots more around the edges of the property. I enjoyed mowing the grass myself, riding the mower back and forth, circling the trees.

No, I didn't! You know Daddy is the gardener. He's the only one who rides the mower. I never disturb nature. I'd never kill living things, like bugs and grass, though everybody else does. Daddy chops off the heads of innocent blades of grass on a regular basis. He plants roses, in penance.

No, of course not! Daddy doesn't believe in penance. He doesn't see anything at all significant about mowing the grass.

Daddy won't deadhead his roses. Once he plants something, he just lets it grow until it's had enough of life and stops growing of its own accord. Except grass. Grass, he mows. Grass was already growing in the lawn when we moved here. He didn't plant it. He has no qualms about mowing it.

I scrubbed the woodwork beside the porch light to remove the evidence that birds once built a nest here. You can't even tell there was a pair of robins working on their hopes. I made up a story about them. Remind me to tell you "The Story of Surprise" next time you're home. Ask me where the nest went. I use the Socratic Method in the story.

I made a soufflé, but when I peeked through the glass door, it was flat. I usually watch it carefully to make sure it doesn't fall, but this time it didn't even rise, so I didn't have to hold my breath and try not to make noise or blink. There was nothing raised there, to keep hoping it would keep holding up. I followed the recipe precisely like I always do. I preheated the oven, slid the pan in, carefully closed the oven door immediately but gently as I've always done. I wanted to surprise Daddy for his birthday with a soufflé. But, there is nothing to be done.

I saw that painted turtle again. At the side of the road, plodding across the shoulder in the direction away from the highway, away from the car tires. I was slowing down just before I pulled in the driveway, and I saw it. I felt guilty about ignoring it this morning as I zipped past it on my way to the store to pick up the milk for coffee I forgot to stop for last night on my way home.

Traffic has been continuous here for all of the past seven minutes. The last car just ahead of me is pulling out of sight around the corner. Nobody stopped to carry this little turtle out of harm's way while I was at the deli. I was not even chatting with the cashier, I was in a hurry to get back.

Yes, this tiny little shell has survived, and without assistance. Was it by pure chance, or through divine providence? In the rear-view mirror, these possibilities always look the same.

I am staring out my driver's-side window at the turtle, as my car continues to roll ahead. I am ignoring the sight through the front windshield, though the pavement is rushing up before me. Nothing else matters but the life of this wee beast, its little legs picking its way over rocks, weaving between dandelions, hovering a bit unsteadily as it navigates the rough terrain, tripping over stems and bent leaves and bitty rocks and clumps of dirt. It looks determined, pursuing the destination it is gravitating towards. I believe it is unconscious as to how it is being directed— by its recognition of a particular scent in the air which wafts here after originating in the vicinity of what the turtle must vaguely recall is the smell of its home.

This morning, stars stayed in the sky after daybreak, a thin stream of dots lining the horizon. Are stars no longer crossing paths with the first rays of the sun? Today they are sullen, merely coexisting. I'm guessing these are not even stars. The satellites are here.

The satellites will watch over you, for your own eternity, and they do not care about us. You might believe they are taking my place, taking over my vigilant watch.

But, I've never left, and I will never leave you. I cannot tear myself away from you. You, alone? On your perilous journey through this universe I created for your ease? No, you will never be alone. I made it wide enough to hold the echo of my laughter. My tears became the ocean where you will gleefully dash into the breakers while you are secretly wishing to be swept away against your will.

Do you know I will be the tide, pushing you back up onto the sand, forever relentlessly lapping the shore, bathing you and caressing your sun-hotted skin to keep you from burning?

Tornado

We promised mother, "Mr. Clean" would swoop out of the bottle in a tornado of housecleaning. My little sister and I had seen him do it, on TV.

"Mr. Clean" resisted the clarion call when I untwisted his lid.

"So, where is he?" asked my mother, her foot tapping the dirty kitchen floor.

The genie's bottle sat silent.

My sister knew he was in there, stubbornly refusing to cooperate. She threw a tantrum, howled into the opening, "You come out of there, this instant!"

Travel Is Broadening

The six-foot monstrosity sat in the corner next to her refrigerator, partially blocking the door to the laundry room. It looked to be mostly brown, a lumpy ball, a collection of organic detritus. Made of woven vines and branches cemented together with some unknown sticky substance, its parts curved in onto itself as if answering its own query as to where it was from.

My friend described the origin of this agglomeration of twigs and trees, bushes and bits of leaves: this dark-colored globe came from deepest Africa, from an actual aboriginal tribe. It's a religious artifact, she explained, stolen from a spot, partially hidden, alongside the path to the hunting grounds. It had become available to outsiders unconnected to the African terrain, through the scheming of the uncouth, much as a special building in Brooklyn might be relieved of a holy scroll or chalice by a heathen or a sinner needing only to turn it into cash as quickly as possible.

The vines and sticks had not been neatly trimmed of their foliage before coming together. Some might be poisonous.

Someone drove a truck into the jungle and hoisted the 500-pound globule into its bed. The bribe had been hefty, she said, but once the relic had been delivered to the nearest city, the robbers could find no takers, so she had obtained it for a song.

Then, there was that matter of the curse. That might have had something to do with the thieves being anxious to be rid of the beast.

It had cost my friend a small fortune to have it shipped from overseas and delivered to her rural cottage in northern New Jersey. But, as she said, "Where on earth are you ever going to find a sculpture like this, or, for that matter, anything covered with the semen of generations of young men?"

Wall

When the Berlin Wall came down, my daughter was four. I wept as I watched young men in tears dancing in the streets, the chains of repression snapping, political oppression evaporating, all unfolding on TV.

I threw a party for my daughter and all her little friends. We had cake and punch, while their mothers enjoyed two hours free. I taught the girls to sing in celebration when something unexpected tilts the axis of the world so it spins a little straighter. I made up a song to the tune of "London Bridge," and we danced and sang, as children do.

The Berlin Wall is falling down,
Falling down,
Falling down,
Falling down.
The Berlin Wall is falling down.
We're so happy!

Then I told them the history, the story I read in the papers of two lovers who had scaled the wall to escape to freedom. As searchlights glinted off barbed wire, they believed the armed lookouts standing on top would see the sparkle in their love-struck eyes and know instinctively what true love deserves, and would let them pass, to start a life together, where they wanted to live.

Hand in hand, hidden only by their dreams, they started running toward the border. No one watching made a sound as they made their breathless dash.

Twenty feet from the end of the yard, one was shot, and dropped to the winter-barren ground. The other dropped, too, and held a golden head and screamed to the universe that this couldn't be true.

And, after a very long while, still twenty feet from freedom, but not rising, the other was shot, too.

They died in each other's arms.

I told the children such walls are relegated to history. Lovers no longer need to fear they might be shot, separated, or forced to live their entire lives apart on opposite sides of a wall:

> *Who knows what friends we will meet someday who now live on the other side? In the past, young girls like you might have lived and died on the wrong side of a wall and never had the chance to meet your one, true love. But you are free to travel the whole world to find the one for you.*

The stories we tell children, that wishes do come true if you blow out all the candles in one breath.

I want to apologize for repeating history. I was young, too, and had never traveled the world beyond the news.

Walt Whitman Has a Stroke in ShopRite

G
ood day, sir!" I say cheerfully to Walt Whitman, and, as he replies with a silent, helpless stare, I realize something is wrong.

I help him to let go of the tomato, unbend the clenched pinky finger holding it fast against his thumb. His other three fingers lay limp, drooped over the orb, having forgotten their purpose in picking up the tomato, which now rests in the top seat of his shopping cart.

Walt stares at his odd right hand, where three of his fingers are not working properly, not responding at all, and his pinky is contracting in a spasm. He tries again to make them work as they normally do.

Like a coin-operated machine with a mechanical toy-grabbing claw, he swings his hand over the metal cage bucket of the shopping cart, where a toddler would sit, buckled in, and drops his hand in the general direction of where the tomato sits, caught in his cart, and not still on the shelf with the other tomatoes. He would pick it up again, except that three of his fingers, of all his body parts, are in complete failure mode. Plus, his pinky looks oddly misshapen and is not responding to his mental commands to relax itself.

Walt takes a quick inventory of his personal facilities. He seems to be thinking okay. The rest of his physiology appears to be under his control and competent. It is only these few fingers that are giving him grief, and he refuses to admit that this minor breakdown will cause him the inconvenience of interrupting his planned evening meal.

Standing next to the shopping cart, determined to complete his task, Walt maneuvers his upper body, hoping to find another way to pick up the tomato and weigh it in his hand to make a determination if this is to be the tomato for tonight's salad or not.

Should he return this tomato to the bin, leave it there for the next customer, and select a new one, or is this the tomato he will slice, lay across his lettuce leaves, cover with sliced onion and dressing, and toss?

Whitman feels a poem coming on, a poem about the melding of the flavors in a salad of individual ingredients, the textures offering an experience once shared by Adam and Eve and all the rest, though without the dressing. People throughout time have been picking from their gardens and masticating their food.

How exquisite to have shared such a mundane activity with Shakespeare, with Milton, with Popes and pimps, queens and minstrels, throughout history and throughout the world. People everywhere and at every time have eaten food, leafy vegetables and more.

But, tomatoes!

Tomatoes are new. Once believed to be poisonous, they now delight the palate, improving every summer dinner along the Eastern seaboard, enhancing the flavor of every other vegetable they come to associate with on the plate.

Walt pauses in his poetic reverie and gets back to the business at hand. He cannot get to his writing desk until he has accomplished the task of shopping. Walt knows what he wants to do. He has got to pick a tomato worth five cents for his salad. He's got to test this tomato and all the tomatoes in the bin until he finds one of the proper weight. He's done this a thousand times without incident.

He notices, this time, it is different. He is not sure what interrupted his day, his routine, but he is pressed for time and must continue. It's getting late, and he is getting hungry.

Tomato. Pick one. He just has to get his body to go along with the idea. Rotating his upper torso in the direction of the tomato and using the muscles of his upper abdomen, which still cooperate, he pushes his arm with his shoulder. But, as his arm makes its horizontal sweep, it drags behind the foolish claw, which has forgotten how to grasp a tomato, this tomato, which is his tomato, unless it comes to weigh too heavily in his palm, in which case he will set it back with the other tomatoes he had already rejected and those he has not yet tried to examine to see if they measure to his satisfaction.

He tries again to pick up the tomato. His body is being silly, non-cooperative. So unlike itself.

Dinner is to be in thirty minutes, if it is to be accomplished on time, and so now he rushes. Walt eyes the tomato in his cart. Is it "his" tomato, or not? He knows he cannot guesstimate its weight and try to figure in his head the change he'll need to pay for it without picking it up, turning it over in his palm, and, pumping his wrist up and down, judge it impartially. His palm will let him know the truth.

The pressure on his palm from the intersection of the formula for gravity, mass, and inertia (he had enjoyed taking measurements with his slide rule in school) will tell him whether this tomato is worth approximately a nickel or not.

If only his fingers would follow the chide of his shoulder and clasp themselves over the tomato, just so, and hold their position and coddle the delicate fruit without bruising it, lift it, hold it just right, and gently toss it, again and again, even just a few times, and catch it in his palm until his brain is ready to say, This one is too light, or This one is too heavy, or This one is just right!

At its first try, Whitman's body had cooperated. He had rejected two tomatoes already, both too heavy. And now, it was his brain that had failed in its duty to manage his extremities in the no-nonsense way Walt had always come to expect. Whitman's brain normally took after his English father, never taking No for an answer, and regularly monitoring every part of his body to assure its musculature was able and its demeanor was cooperative and compliant.

Ah, it is only I who recognize what escapes Whitman's once-keen eye, or, rather, his once-swift brain, as his eye does see the tomato just beyond his grasp. It is his brain that cannot imagine the swirl of iron-rich blood brimming with oxygen-laden cells has been denied passage through the artery to his brain due to a clot, preventing him from figuring in his head the change he'll need to pay for it.

Whitman's insistent push of his arm to the spot where it needs to be but cannot go continues until it is interrupted by his realization he has not yet weighed the tomato, though it is in the top basket of his shopping cart.

He does not know if the nickel in his pocket will cover the cost of the tomato.

He has lost something, something vital, the ability to grasp, lift, and toss a tomato to weigh it properly. Walt gives me a quizzical look. He knows he needs help. If he cannot complete a task as commonplace as collecting a tomato in his hand for the purpose of determining its weight to guarantee its cost does not exceed the value of the coins in his pocket, of which he was sure, he is sure, he'd had when he'd left home to go to ShopRite, then something is amiss. On realizing that this predicament is something beyond his control, Walt attempts to put into words his request for my assistance. On finding himself unable to speak, the poet realizes what it is that has happened.

He says to himself, I believe I am unwell.

Usually when I see Whitman at ShopRite, being the overfamiliar sort of gadabout that I am, but realizing his proud reserve, I merely smile and say, "Good day, sir!" to which he invariably nods and says, "Yes, it is. A very good day indeed!" and we go on about our business, the business of adding things to our separate carts and paying for them, leaving the store, and going about with our lives, individual as they are.

On seeing Whitman struggling with his tomato and trying to vocalize, yet being unable to utter a word, I realize what has happened. I call 911 on my cell and lead him gently to a seated position on the floor. I sit with him to make sure he won't hurt his head if he falls over.

When Pluto Was a Planet

From the time of antiquity, even if everyone else around was insisting on the veracity of some bald-faced lie they had obviously made up, like when alchemists insisted they could spin straw into gold, an astronomer could still be trusted to tell the truth, and to die, if necessary, in defense of the truth. Anyone who looked into a telescope could see what he saw.

And, besides—math. Hello.

Would-be-planet Pluto is again in the news, this time called "an airy kind of mini-mass, sort of like those larger airy maxi-masses we call 'real planets.'" Size, and nothing more, now differentiates Pluto from "planets," who retain their rights as card-carrying members of the elite "Knights Templar of the Solar System (Round-the-Sun) Table," otherwise known as "planets who appear on the standardized test."

I can no longer wrap my intellectual identity around knowing which bits of astromatter circle the Sun in a properly slightly ovalish manner, and which have orbits overly ovalish. It was its exceedingly-odd orbit which first called Pluto's planethood into question, negating the need to measure diameter or airiness of being.

But today, it is not scientists, but the media who decide whether Pluto is a "planet," and they base that decision on the weight of popular opinion.

Without evidence-based science forming our understanding, how can we possibly hope for gender equity, gel that truly whitens teeth, lightning-speed internet access, or any of the modern miracles we'd come to expect the future would bring? Forget the flying cars and the condo on Mars.

And we'll probably end up making concessions on previously hard-earned wins, and give back truths we "know" to be right. Women voting. Flush toilets.

Have you, personally, tried flushing one of the newer "toilets"?

Where Does the Apple Fall?

Their front yard was always burnt with spots of dead grass, where solitary dandelion plants had been drenched with Roundup. There were yellow streaks where nothing grew along the length of the driveway, around the mailbox, around the garden, along the edges of the lawn at the street, around a pile of rocks my dad had collected and stacked in one corner of the property between the stop sign at the intersection and the street sign. Around the well.

My mom laughed at what she called evidence of Dad's one personality aberration, a tendency towards perseverance. When my father developed Alzheimer's Disease, he took to lawn maintenance with a vengeance.

Destroying weeds became his passion. He wanted to do what he could, while he still could, to leave my mother a legacy of his love: a well-maintained property, as well-cared for as ever he cared for my mother, their marriage, and our family. He pruned old trees, cutting branches nearly to the trunk, trimmed bushes neatly to the ground—and he killed weeds.

My father developed lymphoma and died. My mother developed lymphoma and is in hospice.

I live across the street, and I'm preparing to sell their house. I carry the container of Roundup weed killer from my parents' garage to my car and take it to the municipal authority's hazardous waste disposal facility.

As I tie up the last bundle of mom's newspapers for recycling, I read a headline from *The New York Times*, which my parents read faithfully every day of their lives: "Monsanto Ordered to Pay $289 Million in Roundup Cancer Trial."

Whistle

The dorm door was always locked, so her boyfriend would shift his Malibu Classic into park, open his car door, and whistle. Two fingers from each hand stabbed into the corners of his mouth, lips pursed against his front teeth, his tongue skillfully maneuvering the flow of air, expelled with force to pierce the night with shrill alarm to give his girlfriend a heads-up.

She had 43 seconds to jump out of bed, throw on some clothes and sneakers and run down two flights of marble stairs to unlock the front door. They coordinated it exactly, so she would arrive to turn the lock from the inside, just as he arrived from the parking deck and pulled the heavy wooden door open from the outside.

Her boyfriend took time to take one last drag on his Kool. He held his breath and flicked the cigarette to the ground. He twisted it into the macadam with the steel-tipped toe of his brown leather work boot. He would be ready to blow the smoke into her eyes when she opened the door, so her tears of joy when he kissed her would seem cinematic.

A hopeless romantic, he believed her tears for him were real. And they were ... real tears.

When she was longer than 43 seconds—"I couldn't find my other shoe"—she had stolen an extra moment, after kissing her real lover goodbye, to watch him run down the long hallway toward the far stairwell, the one furthest from the parking garage. She hoped he would not be discovered beating a hasty exit.

A hopeless romantic, she sometimes half expected he might pause in his panicked flight, turn, wink, and blow her a kiss.

"Arrivederci, mon amour!"

Women at Work

Linda-Mae Jewel and ... What's-'er-Name?

The Southern Belle beauty, and Good Ol' Plain Jane. I had to choose, from just these two, who would fit our boss's mood and blend into our corporate culture. So far, on the payroll, I was the sole outlier—American and independent, a woman whose presence lent no expectations but of work excellence. This band, a hard-working Asian family, had need of an English speaker—and this was key, one with a brain—and so had hired me.

The leader of our feckless crew happily called me "Sue," which sounded to him like "Hsu," a common name, not strange at all, as if a man in my employ was given the ordinary name of "Jim." "Mim" was how I referred to him, the man who'd hired me after a broken-English interview and a pair of guarantees. I would give him a month, and he gave me three, to see if it all worked out, my working for him, him working with me.

I had proven myself reliant and he, himself, a giant in this world of international trade I was just learning. We each were yearning to make a substantial living in this land of opportunity: a woman fresh from university, and an intelligent businessman. I had no inkling of how they over in Asia were accustomed to thinking about work.

He was smart enough to see I was no ordinary girl. I was not mere window-dressing for his staff, to impress his clientele. His expectations were that we would hire someone new to do the easy tasks we needed done. So, to prove my skill at management, I planned to hire someone to type and fill the orders and answer the phone. I knew a receptionist would have to play the silly game which had no name, so I knew it might be better to pick a girl with experience in working in a business, one who knew the rules and how they get things done, and hopefully she'd find it fun.

My only applicants had both been fired from their previous jobs. Neither would admit to fault but freely spilled on what was wrong with where they'd been. Both blamed their long-term unemployment on a general lack of toleration for their aging. A female's skills were less enchanting if her looks were fading.

Both women were looking to work outside the home, more from loneliness than from financial need. One, a recent widow now living on ample retirement savings, she had herself kept the books for decades at a small family-owned firm. Her spouse and the company that employed her both went under at the same time. Alone at home, she was depressed and feared she'd soon grow weak and sick. She needed to find an occupation that would bring her into daily contact with friendly faces.

The other had refused to perform the tasks asked of her by her corporate manager, as those tasks were never in the original job description and were activities normally required only of ladies of the night employed in the world's oldest profession. Despite typing so quickly the business letters for her important boss in their international corporation, she had not been given a letter of recommendation for her work. Out of spite, she said.

I had no way of knowing whether she was right.

Her husband made plenty of money, so that was not the thing, but she felt unappreciated at home because, to him, his professional status was all. He acted like a king, and expected that she would be his willing servant. They had been married forever, but shared nothing in common but a desire to spend their time in the company of others.

Our company was involved in international trade, but also was small and family-owned, so neither applicant's employment experience offered her an advantage.

In interviews, they opened up in speaking of business sins. In one, the family running the business had had a falling out with the IRS, and that had ended badly. The quick typist's corporate boss had let her go when he'd found a younger lass most willing to perform tasks requiring none of the professional skills one could learn in secretarial school.

I fantasized about their plights. The southern girl, the blonde bombshell, insisted she could type really fast, and insisted that fast was all that mattered. I sensed that her confidence had been shattered. She said she felt a pressure to conform to ordinary social norms for women in her position—a girl who, for all her charms, could not keep wandering fingers and straying arms from grabbing her, pulling her tits, and calling her out for her resistance. Her overly demanding boss had let her go as soon as he'd found a typist who'd meet his not-on-the-job-description requirements without complaining.

The other, older woman knew her looks were gone, but never cared. She answered the phone competently, but she had never had to greet visitors to the office. She conscientiously applied herself to task, and did well. But the small, family-owned company she'd worked for did not last. When the owners retired, all her loyalty could not save her position—her competence and valorous attendance, all in vain when they closed.

Both women seemed surprised, a bit embarrassed, to be found in such a down and lowered employment status. The pretty smile, once so proudly prized, the one that had easily gotten her hired before, was no longer young and sweet enough for her to offer it alone as sufficient evidence of her worth. She stressed that her typing skills were fast, fast and accurate. The other, working hard, above and beyond the call of duty, with the ability to quickly send the product out the door, had seen her dedicated ethic touted while the firm was doing well, but then, when they decided they no longer wanted to be in the business of having things to sell, her services were no longer desired.

Both were desperate for this one position I could offer. Both seemed poised and competent. No hiring manager could fail to see, each could say with perfect confidence, "The perfect person for your job is me!" My crystal ball looked deep into the future, to where my boss was scolding me for bringing on board a worthless bitch or praising my intuition, for hiring the best woman, well-suited for the job.

Both ladies were typists. Both spoke English. Both could be pleasant, though one tried harder. But it all came down to what goes down in an office beyond the written duties of the job.

I looked at these hapless women at my desk. Which would be looked at most fondly by our team and clients, found best to represent us, American Micro Chips, Incorporated? I needed someone who looked the part to fit in with our corporate image. American. A young upstart. But neither of these women fit this category neatly.

I reflected on my need to sate my protector's greed and feed his ego. He was always respectful of the opposite sex, but when his foreign customers came to call, who would they want to see at his side, at his beck and call? I imagined the clients, all male, dealing deals, these macho men preferring their libation, tea, served by a subservient cutie—certainly not me. I never could bring tea with a genuine smile, without an eyeroll or three.

I knew my strengths and my limitations. I could see myself getting fired for saying some honest truth, for blurting out, "You're idiots, you men! I am not Barbie. You are not Ken. This is not pretend. It's real. You want a business deal? Talk to me, not my gorgeous body. Pick my mind, don't fantasize about my naked, hidden plusses.

"And stop gawking at me with your drooling pusses!"

But I was concerned for more than me. I gave so much consideration to how the hiree would be treated. Could she defend herself and hold her head high?

This one could, this girl who was a joy to look at. She was clearly not available to be pawed or toyed with and would not allow herself to be treated as an object. She'd left her last position after demanding recognition for work, not just her looks, and she did not give in to some crude boss's lewd suggestions.

I suggested we hire the typist who looked the part of bait but was not a fish in the sea likely to be caught. She was a gal determined to be master of her fate. If one of the guys should make a pass, she could deflect it. I considered that was good enough. And this was no Solomon's decision. I could not divide this one job into two, to hire one, a hundred-five-words-a-minute typist and perky cutie, and also hire the other, a go-getter who would work hard but would not attract the kind of attention which might boost sales.

Neither needed undue supervision. I could offer only one position, though we held out a reservation, that if another opened up, we'd call on Woman Two.

In the end, it wasn't my call, but, as I'd recommended, we hired the doll, not the widow.

And right away, I regretted my imperfect assessment of the candidates and my recommendation for the hire. This girl who settled into her new position just inside the door of American

Micro Chips, Incorporated could type fast, and did, but quickly drew the line at anything not included in that strict job description. No packing boxes, no adding columns of numbers into totals, no calling travel agents for reservations for intercontinental flights. This flighty girl could type, that much was true. But there was nothing else she was willing to do.

We needed a fast typist. That was too true. When orders had to go to shipment and time was of the essence, her fingers flew across the keyboard. But for the other six-and-a-half hours each day, it would have been nice to have something else for her to do to justify her full-time salary.

Linda-Mae spent two hours at lunch reapplying her makeup, touching up her nails, keeping up the appearance of a working girl and all that that entails.

Months later, at the point of exasperation, I finally discovered Linda-Mae Jewel's one talent, the thing that she alone could do, that, without question, made her indispensable, a valuable, necessary member of our staff. We'd hired a new salesman, who'd taken the position after one look at our charmer, the pretty girl who met him at the front door. Her makeup flawless, her neckline low, her hair perfectly coifed, her closely-fitted skirt neatly pressed, her lipstick fresh—when he winked at her, she winked right back and smiled. He agreed to triple our profits in three months or his salary back.

My boss took a risk and hired this handsome chum, who took Linda-Mae to lunch ... and then some. They'd disappear for three hours in the middle of each afternoon and come back drunk, her hair undone. But, he brought our sales out of their slump. He earned his salary, this chump. Our profits soared.

And, every day, before she left at noon, and then again, when she came back, by three, this professional girl reapplied fresh, red lipstick over a great big smile.

During her quarterly review, we discussed her job performance and I could point to nothing that needed improvement. I relayed my boss's message of commendation, for helping keep up employee morale.

Though we never discussed a raise or additional benefits, and she never requested vacation or more time off, she always looked quite satisfied, pleased as punch.

Thank you for reading *Snow Balls*

AUTHOR

"It's amazing to think Susanna Lee hasn't changed a bit since her yearbook photo."

—no one ever

Susanna Lee is a writer from the rural area in northern New Jersey where drivers stop to give bears crossing the road the right of way. Her work has been published in *brevitas, First Literary Review – East, Sensations Magazine, The Red Wheelbarrow, The Stillwater Review, The World According to Twitter, Voices From Here 2,* and her first book of poetry, *Sunrise Mountain,* 2015, which is now out of print. The volumes of Lee's collected works, published by Rose Mason Press as the *Cubist Poetry Series,* offer the reader a kaleidoscopic view of her writing. The first printing, in 2021, was a "Pandemic Panic!" version. The author was not sure she would not be touched by the contagion, but wanted her admittedly imperfect words to survive: she set them free in haste. She has since reworked the books: proofread and edited, corrected spacing errors, and vanquished typos – at least, most of them – for this 2022 printing. *Snow Balls* consists of short stories, many autobiographical. *Great Blue Heron* is a collection of 5-7-5 haiku arranged in mini-chapbooks on various themes, such as pop culture, nursery rhymes, and art history—and with a bonus: haiku suitable for including in greeting cards on every special occasion. Lee's poems sonnet length and shorter appear in *Twisted Carrot,* poems longer than one page are in *God Laughs*, and her one-page poems are in *My Husband's Roses.* Lee's family recipes are preserved in *Fluffy Muffins*, which includes a section of instructions in kitchen basics for new cooks. Lee celebrates her love of music in bringing to print a newly discovered manuscript written eighty years ago by a friend's uncle, Jerome Bengis. Included with the found monograph, *Beethoven and His Nine Symphonies*, was a Forward by professor of music Edward Dickinson. Bengis' nephew Michael Bengis added a Preface. Lee added an Introduction and an Afterword and gave the book the title *Genius in 9 Symphonies.*

IN GRATITUDE

Thank you to my teachers, my family and friends, my poetry family (my poetry husband—you know who you are—helped me conceive this book) and especially Jim Klein, my poetry sensei. My writing has flourished because of you all: your kindness, technical guidance, generous feedback, patience, and love.

A special thank you to members of my poetry workshops, including fellow poet Jennifer Poteet, who proofread an early draft of this book. (Typos in this current version I've added fresh.)

I have enjoyed hearing featured readers and sharing my work at the open mic at events held at or sponsored by The Red Wheelbarrow Poets, *North Jersey Literary Series, POETRY at the BARN,* Tea NJ, *Thursdays Are For Poetry,* Luna Parc, The Writers' Roundtable of Sussex County, NJ, *Carriage House Poetry Series,* Women Reading Aloud, Poets of the Palisades, Pagoda Writers, Black Dog Books, Hudson Valley Writers Center, Paulenskill Poetry Project, *Tea and Conversation,* Broad Street Books, Silconas Poetry Center of Sussex County Community College, brevitas, the now-defunct Gainville Café, Great Weather for Media, Parkside Lounge, and bookstores, colleges, clubs, and public libraries throughout the Tri-State region.

All you who have shared with me your own poetry and stories from your own life have freed me to share mine.

I'm deeply grateful to all who have invited me to be a featured reader or to speak on the subject of poetry.

I wish to thank the editors who have chosen to include my work in the publications listed below.

Prior Publication

Brookes, Paul, ed. *The Wombwell Rainbow*, blog,
    2020 October 10. https://thewombwellrainbow.com
Crews, David, ed. *The Stillwater Review*, Volume 9. The Betty
    June Silconas Poetry Center, 2019.
Fogarty, Mark, ed. *The Red Wheelbarrow 9*. White Chickens
    Press, 2016.
---. *The Red Wheelbarrow 10*. White Chickens Press, 2017.
---. *The Red Wheelbarrow 11*. White Chickens Press, 2018.
---. *The Red Wheelbarrow 12*. White Chickens Press, 2019.
---. *The Red Wheelbarrow 13*. White Chickens Press, 2020.
---. *The Red Wheelbarrow Poem of the Week*. White Chickens
    Press, 2017.
---. *The Red Wheelbarrow Poem of the Week*. White Chickens
    Press, 2017.
---. *The Red Wheelbarrow Poem of the Week 2*. White Chickens
    Press, 2018.
---. *The Red Wheelbarrow Poem of the Week 3*. White Chickens
    Press, 2019.
---. *The Red Wheelbarrow Poem of the Week 4*. White Chickens
    Press, 2020.
LeBlanc, Jean, ed. *Voices From Here 2*. The Paulenskill Poetry
    Project LLC, 2017.
MacLeod, Selene, and Jordan Gallader, eds. *Anthem: A Tribute
    to Leonard Cohen*. Nocturnicorn Books, 2017.
Messineo, David, ed. Dance, *Sensations Magazine*,
    Supplement 9. David Messineo, 2019.
---. Decade of Dichotomy, Feb. 1, 2011 – Jan. 31, 2021,
    Sensations Magazine, Supplement 11. David Messineo,
    2021.
---. Global Warming, *Sensations Magazine*, Supplement 10.
    David Messineo, 2020.
---. The Gathering Storm, *Sensations Magazine*, Supplement 6
    David Messineo, 2017.
---. Westward Expansion, 1784-1959, *Sensations Magazine,*
    Supplement 8. David Messineo, 2019.

Pogue, David. *The World According to Twitter*. Black Dog & Leventhal, 2009.

Redus, Glenn, ed., *The Shinbone Star*, blog, 2020 March 23. https://exjournalistsunite.wordpress.com

Sostchen-Hochman, Cindy, and Karen Neuberg, eds. *First Literary Review – East*. September 2019. http://www.rulrul.4mg.com/

The 14th Annual brevitas Festival of the Short Poem. First Street Press, 2017.

The 15th Annual brevitas Festival of the Short Poem. First Street Press, 2018.

The 16th Annual brevitas Festival of the Short Poem. First Street Press, 2019.

The 17th Annual brevitas Festival of the Short Poem. First Street Press, 2020.

Winners of The White Shoe Haiku Contest, *The White Shoe Irregular*, 2000 November 27. http://www.whiteshoe.org/archive/001127haiku1.html

Winners of The White Shoe Haiku Contest, *The White Shoe Irregular*, 2001 January 16. http://www.whiteshoe.org/archive/001127haiku1.html

Published by Rose Mason Press

Sunrise Mountain: Haiku and Other Poetry
by Susanna Lee

Twisted Carrot: Petite Poems
by Susanna Lee

My Husband's Roses: One-Page Poems
by Susanna Lee

God Laughs: Longer Poems
by Susanna Lee

Great Blue Heron: Haiku
by Susanna Lee

Snow Balls: Short Stories
by Susanna Lee

Fluffy Muffins: Recipes for My Peeps
by Susanna Lee

Genius in 9 Symphonies: How Beethoven Reinvented Music
by Jerome Bengis

Please gift a Rose Mason Press title to someone you love.